To

The Warm Presence

and all those who help us

here on the Earth.

Preface

After my first book was published, *Beyond the Sallagh Braes*, a memoir of my life and travels, I realised there was a reason to write a second one. I had left a lot of things unsaid. My purpose in writing this book has been to make sense of the Spiritual Journey I found myself on while navigating my way through a busy world. I felt the need to tell people of my discoveries while researching everything that had previously been a mystery to me. Most of all I wanted to express my thanks to God, the Angels and all in Spirit for helping not only me, but everyone on the Earth.

Throughout the book I have named God as the Creator. I am well aware that others will use different names, such as the Divine, Source, The Universe and many more. We must all use the term we feel most comfortable with to describe the warm presence that dwells within and around us.

It has never been my intention to convert anyone to my beliefs, we must all be free to have our own thoughts and walk our own path. Once I began to research information to form my beliefs I was amazed at how quickly guidance came to me. I got a sense of knowing the answers to my questions or I would find myself in the right place at the right time.

Meditation has been the most useful key on my Spiritual Journey. Someone once said, "Prayer is when we talk to God, meditation is when God talks to us." I believe they were right. When we become aware of the Angels in meditation we have a direct line to the help and wishes of our Creator.

This is the story of my path up the mountain so far. As I take one more step along the way may I always be kind to others and grateful for my life here on our beautiful Earth. I think kindness and gratitude are what bring us happiness but greater than these is Love. When Love fills our heart there is no room for anything else. When we share that love with others it comes back to us tenfold.

Contents

Destiny 1

My Grandmother 8

My Mother 15

My Story 22

Energy Awareness 42

A Time of Change 49

Going to America 56

Meeting the Love of My Life 59

Getting Married and Going to Sea 64

Becoming a Little Family 72

Visiting Fortune Tellers 78

Returning to Work 85

The House with the Stunning Views 89

The Castle 94

Country House Accommodation 101

The Unexpected Guest 111

Moving to Spain 115

Returning to Northern Ireland 120

Reiki 130

- Angel Awareness Classes 135
- Discoveries on My Journey 140
  - Crystals 140
  - Aura Soma 142
  - Colour Workshop 143
  - Music 144
- Decluttering 146
- Dreams 156
- Angel Meditations with Mary 158
- Glastonbury 162
- Return to Spain 168
- A Time of Reckoning 182
- Acknowledgements 191
- About The Author 193

Destiny

He was a big man, what my father would have called a good build of a man.

We sat together in his little cell like room. It was cell like not only because of its size but also because of the dim light. There were two straight backed chairs, one facing the other. To one side of them was a covered table, on top of it, a beautiful Moroccan lantern was casting patterns, intricate patterns of light, on the walls. Beside the lantern sat a yellow sphere of some sort of opaque crystal, or maybe stone. Behind me, pushed against a wall, was a couch with a minimal frame of wood. It was certainly not built for comfort.

I was nervous as I looked at the carafe of water and glasses the man set on the table. I studied him. He was dressed in black — black trousers and T-shirt and although he had a shaven head, he had a full white moustache of the style I had seen the men in Belgium wear. In the dim light of the room, his face was illuminated. It would have been hard to put an age to him. I decided he was probably in his forties, which meant he was around the same age as me. He could have passed for a Buddhist Monk, he moved with such grace.

I was wondering about the strange fragrance of incense in the room when I realised he was speaking. His voice was soft, gentle, caring, as if he was speaking to a child. There was something familiar about it, and yet it was the first time I had been to this old Spanish house in the centuries' old Spanish village.

On my arrival the character and charm of the house had been obvious. From the narrow, cobbled street, I had admired its neat appearance; the walls painted in pale salmon pink and the black window grills filled with an array of green plants. I used the black, wrought-iron ring to knock on the heavy wooden door, which was set into the thick walls. As I listened to the welcoming bark of the dogs, the door opened slowly and a smiling Asian man invited me to come in and wait. A little later the man wearing black appeared, and after introducing himself as Kenny, he asked me if I would please follow him. On entering, the room was palatial, with high ceilings, terracotta-painted walls, and cream tasselled drapes. I could see at a glance that it housed wonderful treasures from all over the world. Someone in this house had amazing taste in interior design. I followed the man up the Moroccan tiled staircase.

He was sitting opposite me, his knees inches from

mine, his eyes looking intently at my face. Laying his hands loosely in his lap in a relaxed manner he looked very much at home. There was something familiar about him. Did he perhaps remind me of a priest from my childhood?

He spoke, and I paid attention, "Why have you come to see me?" he asked. There was a moment's hesitation before I answered, even though I had rehearsed what I would say before I came. "I haven't been well, and someone recommended I come to see you. I have been told that you are a Healer but you can also see into the future." Then my perfectly rehearsed dialogue left me. "Perhaps you could read the Tarot Cards for me or something," I babbled. He threw back his head and laughed. His laughter reverberated around the small room. "You don't need the Tarot Cards and neither do I, give me your hands and I will tell you what you want to know. I am a Medium and that means that Spirit uses me as a channel for Healing." He asked me if I was alright to continue. I was surprised by what he had just said but knew I could trust this man with my life. He had the kindest eyes. There was something about him. He was professional in his manner, and it gave me the confidence to go on.

"Yes, we will continue," I said. He took my hands and turned them palm-side-up. They dropped naturally to rest on my legs. He hovered his hands above them and closed his eyes. I closed mine too. I don't know why I did so, but it seemed to be the right thing to do. Time stood still. The room was quiet. He spoke softly, "You do not know what is wrong with you?" My voice was little more than a whisper when I replied, "No, I don't." I opened my eyes and noticed a gentle smile on his face. He said, "You are a Healer. This gift has been passed down through the female side of your family. Once you start using the healing energy to help others, it will not build up in your body as it has done now, causing you problems." I gasped and quickly looking down I said, "Oh, my hands, they have been very hot and there has been a tingling feeling, like pins and needles in them, for some time." I stared at my upturned hands and suddenly felt humble. I was just an ordinary girl. I felt emotional and wondered why I had been chosen for this work. Had this been the reason complete strangers had confided personal details about their lives to me? Had they sensed something in me that I didn't even know was there myself?

He was speaking again, "The Gift was passed from your grandmother to your mother but she wasn't well enough to take it. I think you got a double dose!" He described my maternal grandmother and told me of a time when I was a little girl, staying with her for my summer holidays. She didn't have any toys in her house, but he described the little wooden Russian doll in her sewing box that I loved taking apart as a child.

He reminded me of another occasion at her cottage in the Sallagh Braes in County Antrim, Northern Ireland, when I had been taken outside to see the Northern Lights. How could this man whom I had never met before know these things about me unless my grandmother who had been dead for over thirty years was somehow communicating with him? The information he gave me convinced me that there is life after death and the realisation brought a certain joy to me.

He asked me if I would like him to channel healing to me, and, of course, I said yes. I felt warmth and a feeling of Love from the energy coming through his hands, which he held a few inches from me. I began to feel more relaxed than I had for some time. I asked if he would show me how he worked with this healing energy and he said he would be happy to. He gave me instruction on prayer, meditation and healing. Looking at my watch, I was surprised to find that two hours had passed since I had entered the little cell-like room. He stood and I knew our time for this visit was over. I made another appointment to come again, but next time it would be for further instruction on how to pass healing to others.

I came away stunned and exhilarated by the news

I had been given. Standing in the narrow cobbled street in the afternoon sun, about to telephone my husband to come and collect me, a thought came to me. The Healer had talked of Guardian Angels and how they are with us from before we come to the Earth until they take our spirit safely home to our Creator when our physical body dies. During this time, they never leave our side for a moment. I realised that I would never feel alone again, and it was a comforting thought.

Why had I been chosen to walk this path? I asked myself this question over and over again, not only in the coming weeks but in the coming years. Was I like the man I had just met? Could I sense those who were on the other side? Did the word Spirit mean Father, Son and Holy Spirit? Did it encompass the Angels? What about those who had passed over from the Earth? My mind was full of questions. Where were the answers to come from? I didn't realise it then, but I had begun a Spiritual Quest, one that would remain with me for the rest of my life. I was to receive some of the answers, but God willing I shall be given all of the answers when I leave this mortal coil.

For the time being I decided that looking at the bigger picture can be overwhelming. It is manageable if broken down into small parts. I would begin by thinking about how I had inherited this wonderful but unexpected gift.

My Grandmother

I thought about what the Healer had said about this gift being passed down from my grandmother. She had passed away when I was about eleven years old. I could still see her in my mind's eye. She was a big woman, not only in size but in personality. Her dark hair was pulled back in a bun and kept in place with a hair net. Seldom without a smile on her face, her pale blue eyes sparkled. She was full of fun and full of love for everyone she met. She was so kind she would have given you her last crust of bread and she was well thought of by all who knew her.

Her little whitewashed cottage with its door and window frames painted green was as pretty as a picture. It had the magnificent backdrop of the Sallagh Braes in County Antrim and an unrivalled view of the sea. Looking back, I think it may have been known as a tied cottage. It belonged to the people in the big farmhouse where my grandmother worked. When I stayed with her as a child, I remember her taking me to work with her. The green ferns growing on the hillside were beautiful in summer, but later when they changed to bracken they used to scratch my legs on the way up the hill; maybe that is why I remember them so well. It was the 1960s, and I was too young to know or care if she paid rent for the cottage or whether she was allowed to stay there because she worked for the owners. When she finished work, she would hold my hand on the way down the hill, her other hand swinging the little white enamel creamery can of milk, its blue-edged lid firmly in place. Sometimes we would stop to gather wild mushrooms which she roasted in a pan with a little butter when we got home.

My mind had drifted back easily to that time, and I could almost have forgotten the reason I had started thinking about her. I had been looking for clues because of the Healer telling me she had the Gift. What was different about her?

I remember her saying her prayers every night, no matter how tired she was. She had a great belief in God, not the hellfire and brimstone version of Him that people preached over the years. Her God was one of Love, one who would provide for his children. It may have been because of her faith that she always had enough food in the house to share with others.

She worked hard, not only for the owners of the farm but also in her little cottage. On wash day she would begin by separating the coloured laundry from the white sheets, tea towels etc. and then she would boil the whites in a big pot on the stove. A small tin bath and a wash board were brought in from the shed and placed on the kitchen table. She used to scrub everything until she was satisfied it was clean. After rinsing her washing in clean water, which was carried in buckets from the little spout of spring water up the road, everything would be hung outside on the clothesline with dolly pegs to dry. I used to help her to fold the sheets before she aired them on the rack above the stove, later she ironed them and stored them in the big chest of drawers until they were needed.

After a busy day and an evening meal she would tell me it was time for bed. I would snuggle up beside her in the black metal framed bed with brass balls shining on the four corners of it. The mattress was filled with feathers; I know this because they sometimes escaped through the black and white striped cover. The bed was cosier than my bed at home. The bottom sheet was made from cotton flour bags which my grandmother bleached and sewed together by hand. (I now know that a lot of women did this because of the shortages after the war.) The top sheet was lovely and soft. It had pink, blue and white stripes, and it looked really pretty, but on the top of it there was an itchy grey blanket. She told me it was an army blanket, but that didn't mean anything to me at the time. I was born in 1955, and I was too young to know that the blankets had been issued to soldiers who fought in the Second World War. On top of everything else, there was an eiderdown: it was a puffy quilt with a pattern on it, but it was not like the duvets we know today. A long pillow called a bolster and two feather pillows with what I now know to be embroidered white linen pillowcases completed her comfortable bed.

There was a shiny brass oil lamp on the chest of drawers beside the bed and she put it out last thing at night. Before she did so she would give me a sweet, take one herself and read me a story from the children's page in her magazine — or, she would tell me a story. When she finished she would say "Cuddle into my back now and go to sleep, I am going to say my prayers." I would lie for a little while and look at the pink roses on the wallpaper. My father and my uncle had wallpapered the room for her. There was a feeling of love as my grandmother said her prayers and although the brass lamp with its glass shade smelt of paraffin oil there was a lovely glow in the room. Sleep would overcome me and the next thing I knew it was morning and the sun was streaming in through the thick lace curtains on the little sash windows of the cottage. Sometimes I didn't want to leave the cosiness of my grandmother's bed, but her voice calling from the kitchen telling me my porridge was ready soon had me up and getting dressed.

Was there anything else apart from her kindness and faith in God that gave a clue to the fact that my grandmother might have had the gift of healing or seeing into the future? I was back in her little cottage. I imagined the warmth from her stove. I heard her laughter. I can't explain it, but it was as if I had been transported back in time.

Family and friends came to the cottage often, and tea and home-baked bread was given to everyone. I remember my grandmother reading the cards for some of them. She wore a black flowery overall that crossed over at the front and tied. She kept her cards in the pocket of it, they weren't Tarot Cards. They were ordinary playing cards like the ones the family and friends played with at night in her home. I don't ever remember them playing for money, but sometimes they took three matches each from the box of Swan Vestas on the kitchen table. Before a game they each put one in the middle, and at the end of the game the winner got all of them. At the end of the night the matches were put back in the box. It had just been a way of keeping the score.

My grandmother could sometimes be coaxed to read the cards, and some of the people who visited asked her to tell their fortune. It was all about seeing into the future and giving them hope of better times to come. They told her their problems and she gave them advice. Thinking about it now, it was more like a counselling session really. She didn't take money for this. She was a wonderful woman and when her time came to leave the Earth, many years later, God was good to her; she passed away in her sleep. All of her family were heartbroken, and we missed her terribly when she went to join the God she had prayed to so often.

She didn't have a lot of money, but she left me her jewellery box. It was a tartan shortbread tin containing a few strings of beads my grandfather had bought her and various little treasures like her WRVS badge. My mother told me it meant Women's Royal Voluntary Service. My grandmother had played her part for the war effort as many women did during World War II. Her wedding ring, a plain band of rose gold, was left to my mother on condition it went to me after her death. As an adult I watched the film *Lord of The Rings* and thought about how I came to have her ring. After meeting the Healer and hearing his words, I thought about it again. Did great responsibility come with the ring? My grandmother had been psychic, of that there was no doubt, and she also had the ability to make others feel better about themselves. When she had said she was leaving the ring to my mother and later it was to be passed on to me, had she known the special gift that had been bestowed upon her would come to us?

Would we find it a blessing as she had done? I have no doubt she must have thought of it as a blessing because it had brought so many friends into her little cottage and into her life. It had brought great respect from all who knew her as well.

My Mother

I thought of my mother and wondered about her destiny if what the Healer had said was true. My mother didn't read the cards, but she was very astute. It was almost as if she knew things about people without them telling her. She knew what way things would work out in a situation, and I could never get away with anything. People had been known to ask her if she was psychic, and she didn't like it. She had a fear of being that way, I think.

She was a beautiful woman, my mother. The combination of brown curly hair and pale blue eyes suited her, and when she wore her pink lipstick I knew I wanted to look like her when I grew up. She married my father, who was a farmer at heart, and she married into a lifetime of hard work. They raised seven children, who were just like steps of stairs. Times were hard, and money not so plentiful. There was a great deal of love between them, and I suppose that saw them through those times. As far as good looks went, my father was a great match for her. He was tall and well-built, with dark hair, brown eyes and the whitest teeth you could imagine. He could often be serious and quiet, but that is not surprising considering the responsibilities involved in bringing up a big family. When we were visiting others, or when we had visitors at home, he was relaxed and smiled and laughed more. He was well respected, and people sought his opinion often. I suppose you could say he was what was known locally as 'level headed.' In other words, he had a great deal of common sense.

We loved him, and although we had been given our dinner before he came home from work in the evenings, we gathered around him and were delighted if he gave us something from his plate. He was ambitious, always wanting a better home for the family. As a result, we moved house more than most people. He never drank alcohol nor smoked cigarettes as he saw those things as a great waste of money. My mother went along with his ideas, which was something most woman did in those days, the man being seen as head of the household.

My mother on the other hand had a great personality. She was very sociable and loved people as much as my grandmother had. She liked nothing better than someone calling to visit. The kettle would be put on for tea and there would be much talk and laughter for an hour or so. She also liked to tell her children stories about her childhood and her life in general. Also, having been part of a big family, she never seemed to run out of stories to tell. I listened very carefully when she told those stories. While she talked, I sometimes felt sad and at other times happy, but I loved hearing the stories because they gave me an insight into her life when she was young. When she was little more than a child, she had worked for a local farmer. She was at the top of the threshing machine throwing the sheaves of corn into it when one of the farm workers threw a nest of little pink mice at her. She was so afraid she jumped from the top of the threshing machine to the ground. The fear of mice remained with her all her life. When she was old enough, she went to work for an old lady who tested her honesty. My mother had been washing the household linens and clothes when she discovered half a crown in the pocket of the old lady's apron. She immediately gave it to its rightful owner, who said, "I knew it was there and now I know I can trust you." My mother's stories helped to pass many an afternoon by the fire.

Another story she told springs to mind. As a young chambermaid she worked in Ballygally Castle Hotel. Within the castle was a room known as the Ghost Room because it was said to be haunted. It was very popular with honeymoon couples. My mother said the members of staff were so afraid they would only go to work in it if they were in pairs. I could imagine how it must have felt for a sixteen-year-old girl with a vivid imagination. I asked if she ever saw the ghost, but she said she didn't stay in the room long enough. She did her work as quickly as possible and made sure she was never left alone in it. Looking back, I can see she was a great storyteller. I paid attention to her facial expressions and her every word.

Although she herself had been brought up in the country, she was not from farming stock. However, she had a way with animals, and she certainly was not afraid of hard work. She worked hard on the farm and never complained about the amount she had to do. This seems strange to me now when I realise how often she must have been pregnant during the time we lived there. The doctor once asked her why she was having children all the time, laughing, she told him that we had no electricity and therefore no television to pass the time. He laughed with her, but since this was before the contraceptive pill was widely available, he probably understood her situation well. She adored my father and did everything she could for him, even polishing his shoes and setting out his shaving brush, razor and hot water in the mornings. When she prepared the meals he was given the best food in the house; the boys came next, then the girls and finally herself if there was enough left by then. It was the same system in most of the farmhouses around us at meal times.

She could be strict also and took no nonsense from us. Whether it was something going back to her childhood, I have no idea, but the Bible was brought out now and again. Not only for the purpose of reading it, but if she thought we were lying about something we were told to swear on it that we were telling the truth. She told us if we told a lie with the Bible in our hand Old Nick would get us. Even the bravest of us owned up to whatever we had done in case the devil really would get us.

Was she religious? Yes, in her way she was. She was a great woman for teaching us our prayers; not only did she pray, but she expected the same of us. Prayers were said in our house at bedtime every night. My mother would sit on the bed and prompt us in a kind loving way if we forgot something. If our upbringing was strict, I would be the first to admit it was also a happy home and none of us got into any kind of trouble. This was a miracle considering there were seven of us. She loved it when people told her, "Those children are a credit to you." Her home was a credit to her as well as it was kept spotlessly clean, and the children also played their part in keeping it that way.

Years later, when my grandmother passed away suddenly, it broke my mother's heart. Her health deteriorated, and it was a long time before she was well again. For a while she had what was known as a problem with her nerves; in other words, she was emotional. I think it would be fair to say she was grieving. She had good days and bad days. Eventually, she became more like her old self. When the children were almost grown up, the two youngest being fourteen and thirteen, my mother decided to leave home. She moved across the sea, and, for a time, she had fun in her life, but it was short lived because she missed her children. They went to visit her for holidays, but soon she moved back to the area they lived in so she could be near them. My father was devastated when he and my mother broke up, but in the future he went on to marry again. He chose a lovely woman, and she loved the family as much as they loved her. We were glad when my father found happiness. My mother found a new partner too, and eventually she got married again. Her husband worshipped the ground she walked on. Some people may think it is surprising, but my parents and their new partners became friends. That friendship was to last for the rest of their lives. I am glad that they behaved like adults for the sake of the family.

Was my mother psychic or did I feel she was a Healer? I don't know, but the Healer was right in saying she wasn't well enough to take the Gift. The day my grandmother died, her wedding ring passed to my mother and she wore it until she parted from my father. At that point she gave her rings to the family, and she gave me my grandmother's ring. Did the Gift come with it? I put it on my finger, and I have worn it since the day I was given it. Does this mean I am a psychic and a healer? Let me tell you my story and you can decide for yourself.

My Story

I was born in 1955, and my parents brought me home from hospital to my grandmother's house where she placed me in a drawer which she had made up as a cot for me. That was my bed until my father brought the pram home a couple of days later. I remember the high black bouncy pram well because not only was it to serve me, but also the other six children who were my brothers and sisters when they came into the world. My mother, father and I lived with my grandmother for a little while before moving to the town. During that time, my grandmother looked after me while my mother and father worked in the town. My mother worked in a weaving factory and my father in a furniture shop. By caring for me and allowing my parents to work, my grandmother gave them a good financial start to their married life. Working enabled them to buy a terraced house in the town and later they were able to afford a second one. I am not quite sure when we moved to my father's family farm. My paternal grandmother had been living there and she moved to one of the houses my parents owned in the town. All I remember really of that time is starting the little country school near the farm at age four.

My childhood was happy on the farm, especially when my siblings arrived one after the other to keep me company. We had lots of freedom with our time being spent mostly outdoors and, apart from the usual childhood illnesses, like mumps and measles, we were very healthy. Our life was ruled by the seasons as was the life of all the country children. My father kept a lot of sheep with a few cattle and poultry on our farm, which was situated in the Antrim hills. There were quite a few acres of hill farm, with a few fields for grazing cattle and meadows for hay for winter fodder.

The farmhouse was built of stone. The walls were thick, to keep it warm in winter and cool in summer, I suppose. However, in the depths of winter we looked forward to Spring, when it would be warm enough to play outside instead of gathering around the kitchen stove for warmth.

The brighter days always lifted my father's mood. He hated the dark days and the threat of snow. He had lost quite a few sheep in the winter of 1962/63, the year of the big snow, and he had dreaded the onset of winter since then. Darkness descended as early as 4pm and remained until 8am the following morning. As well as working on the farm, he also worked in a shop in the town. It was dark when he left for work in the morning, smartly dressed in his sports coat and flannels, clean shirt and tie. Quite often he wore a Fairisle pullover under his jacket for extra warmth. A heavy overcoat which we all referred to as his topcoat was added when the weather was really cold. He looked handsome and usually left home with a smile on his face. It was dark when he returned at night. He came home, changed into his old working clothes and ate the dinner my mother had prepared for him. Lighting the hurricane lamp, he would go about his chores on the farm. There were many nights when he burst through the door, his outdoor clothes soaking wet or covered in snow. As he kicked the snow from his boots before entering, I am now ashamed to say I wished he would close the door to stop the cold getting in.

My mother had done as much as she could with the animals before he came home but he always liked to keep a check on them especially at lambing time or when the cows were due to calve. I remember thinking I would hate to be a farmer like my father. I wasn't very old when I decided I would not marry a farmer when I grew up because my mother had to work too hard and go out in the cold. It was no wonder we all looked forward to the warmer days of spring.

We eagerly awaited the beginning of March to see

what the weather was like. There was an old saying among the country people, "If March comes in like a lion, it will go out like a lamb." Unfortunately, the reverse could also be true. My father had a book called *Old Moore's Almanac* which he got his information from. I don't think he had a lot of time for psychic predictions, apart from it. It gave him weather forecasts and the best times to sow and reap etc. In many ways, the farmers lived by it, following the phases of the moon for all they did. By not doing so now perhaps we do not have the same affinity with nature. The old wireless which contained a big Exide battery gave us the daily weather forecasts as well as the news, plays and songs from the singers of the day like Gracie Fields, Bridie Gallagher, Val Doonican and also the Showbands before pop music took over the radio waves. My mother happily sang along with these songs as she rocked the most recent baby to sleep. I can still remember the words of those songs to this day.

We always think the weather was better in spring and summer back then than it is now. I remember getting sunburnt one time on the 17th of March, St. Patrick's Day. This was an important day on the farmers' calendar for a different reason. It was the day when, weather permitting, most farmers would plant their potatoes. Still the staple diet in Ireland, they would be planted on 17th March and dug on the

12th of July. My father always said that no potatoes ever tasted as good as the ones you grew yourself. Anyway, potatoes could not have been further from my mind that day. It was sunny and I was lying on a mossy bank at the side of our lane picking violets and playing, as children do. Sun creams weren't used much then as the dangers of getting skin cancer were either not known or not talked about. That evening when I was going to bed my little back was red and sore. My mother covered it in a pink lotion which didn't smell very nice. It was Calamine Lotion and it took the sting out of the burning and soothed my skin. Days later the skin peeled off, and, although it was no longer painful, I learned to be careful when I was outside in the sunshine.

In every farm house, there were a few cures for everyday ailments. Disinfectant was used to wash cuts and grazes. Germolene ointment was put on the clean wounds with a bit of gauze and a bandage, if they were bad enough to merit that level of care. Warm olive oil was the cure for a sore ear. Poultices made from bread soaked in hot water and sprinkled with baking soda were cooled and put on anything that looked as if there was an infection present. This was bandaged and left on overnight to see if it would draw the poison out. There was usually a bottle of Milk of Magnesia for constipation and a bottle of Cod Liver Oil which was said to be good for you. It tasted dreadful. When we had been sick and started to get our appetite back my mother gave us something called panada, it was white bread soaked in warm milk, with a sprinkling of granulated sugar on top. It was not possible to be running to the doctor every five minutes in those days, unless it was something that the old fashioned cures could not heal. It didn't cross my mind that my mother was a healer when she dispensed these old fashioned remedies with a hug, but perhaps she was.

Spring brought the arrival of lambs and it was wonderful to see them gambolling in the fields, their little tails wagging as they fed from their mothers. Sometimes we had a pet lamb to bottle feed if the mother had died giving birth. Spring cast her green mantle over the Earth and the flowers started popping up, first the snowdrops and then the crocus. Daffodils grew in profusion on top of the old wall at the back of the house near the row of stone out buildings. Birds sang and built nests. Hares and rabbits were often seen when we were going for a walk on the hillside, and nature seemed more obvious than it had been in the previous months.

Easter came and the Circuit of Ireland Rally passed the end of our lane, where we gathered, like most of the other families, to watch the cars speed past. I don't know what the drivers thought of the little country children and their parents cheering them on. It was a time when the Catholic families in the area went through Lent. Pancake Tuesday was a day of feasting on homemade pancakes dripping with melting butter and granulated sugar, and this was followed by Ash Wednesday, the beginning of Lent. As a child I was too young to understand the real meaning behind it, all I knew was that my school friends had to give up something they liked. They usually gave up sweets. Even though I was a Protestant attending the only primary school in the area, which was Catholic, I joined them in their sacrifice.

As I grew older, I discovered more about Lent. It is the period of 40 days that runs between Ash Wednesday and Easter Sunday. It is a time in the Christian calendar to focus the thoughts on Christ, the sacrifice he made for us on the cross and His resurrection. During Lent people abstain from something they enjoy and make a donation of money to the church to be used to help others. What they sacrifice varies from one person to another. Quite often it would have been alcohol, cigarettes, sweets, cakes — anything that was a challenge for them to give up.

Easter Sunday was a day when we had a special dinner with lamb or chicken and roast potatoes, followed by Bird's Trifle for dessert — pudding, as we called it then. We had chocolate Easter eggs and we followed the tradition of rolling hard boiled eggs in the afternoon. Having geese, ducks and hens on the farm meant we always had plenty of eggs. My mother hard boiled them for us, sometimes dying them yellow with the blossom from the Whin bushes that grew in profusion on the hillsides. We painted the eggs or put decorations on them with pens, usually drawing little faces on them. Then it was time to roll them down the hill and see whose egg won the race. We would pick them up at the bottom, their little faces cracked, while we argued as to which one was the winner.

I remember having to call with the old lady who lived in a little house at the end of our lane after school one day to give her a message from my mother. She was brushing the flour off the griddle with a goose's wing in preparation for baking soda bread, but she smiled when she saw me. After I had delivered the message, she said, "Go into the porch and bring me the bag of Easter Eggs till I give you one." Well, I searched that porch thoroughly and I could not find those Easter Eggs! I returned to her and explained that they were not there. Smiling, she said, "April Fool." I had no idea what she was talking about until my mother told me later that people play tricks on each other on the first day of April. I thought the lady had been very cruel and my mother said she agreed with me.

After the Easter holidays, we went back to school, and, apart from getting a soaking because of the odd April shower, it was a pleasant walk to it and also going home again at three o'clock in the afternoon. The grass verges on both sides of the road were covered in dandelions and buttercups — or, were they celandines? I never could tell the difference. Wild roses or briar roses, as some people called them, appeared in the hedges, their beauty heralding summer.

I was late coming home from school one day and my mother came looking for me. The little boy from the next farm was getting me one of these roses and my mother told me off for not coming straight home. She made me blush when she told anyone who would listen about my boyfriend getting me a Bucky rose from the hedge.

Spring blended into summer and the days were getting increasingly warmer, the skies bluer and the evenings clear way past ten o'clock. We were always excited to see the first of the swallows arriving back from their long winter holiday in the south. They built nests where the points of the gable met the roof of the old stone farmhouse. Bees, insects and butterflies appeared again as soon as the sun had warmed the Earth.

It was a busy time on the farm, especially for my father; there was so much to do. I remember the family going to the Moss, the local name for the peat bog. My father cut the turf and when it had been lying in the sun for a while, the children played their part by stacking them up on their ends to dry, they looked like little tepees. Later in the summer it was bagged and taken home in my father's van to supplement the winter fuel.

When we stopped for a break at the Moss my father would break the big fruit bun — bread with dried fruit and peel — into pieces and hand us a piece each. After we finished eating it, we would take the bottle he had brought and fill it with peaty water from the little river that ran through the Moss. It was a bit brown in colour, but it tasted fine.

I have heard the English people talk about tickling trout, but my father called it gineling. He would lie down on the bank of the river, cup his hands and place them under the bank and wait patiently. He always ended up catching a couple of trout for tea. It was something he had learned to do as a boy, and he was good at it.

The sheep needed to be clipped, and, without electricity on the farm in those days, my father had to do it with sheep shears. It was warm work. I remember him bent over, wrestling with a ewe, little rivulets of perspiration running down his suntanned forehead. Becoming too hot, he would take off his shirt and continue his work wearing his white vest — or singlet, as some people called it. By the time he finished shearing, it was only fit for the bin. Later the fleeces would be rolled up and taken away to be sold. A good price brought him home with a happy smiling face.

Next came the time for making hay, weather permitting. My father relaxed a little once the haymaking process was complete. The hay was cut, turned, dried and made into rucks — and later, larger pikes — and was saved for feeding the animals in winter. We helped as children and then shared the picnic my mother brought to the hay field. There was tea and sandwiches made from plain sliced bread with tinned corned beef, chopped ham, cheese, beef paste or whatever she had handy. Instead of tea, the children had Creamola Foam. It was made from a tin of something that looked like sherbet dip and when the powder was added to water, it fizzed up. I can still taste it as I write. I can only remember us having two flavours — raspberry and orange.

After the haymaking, my parents took us for the odd day out. These were rare as there was always plenty to do on the farm when my father had a Tuesday off from his other job. We managed to get to the beach or for a run up the coast in the car for an ice-cream. Sometimes we took a picnic to the Sallagh Braes and the children climbed the hills while my mother and father lay on a blanket and sunbathed reading newspapers like the *Larne Times*, *Weekly*

News, or, on a Sunday, *The News of the World*, which we as children were not allowed to read. Lying in bed one night I overheard my mother read a story from it to my father. The headline was 'Have You Ever Heard of a Ghost That Shaves?' I don't remember much about it, but I remember being terrified by it for a long time after that.

We had visits to our grandmothers as well. My father's mother, who lived in the town, had a TV set, which was a novelty to us. The picture was black and white until someone gave my grandmother a sheet of something that looked like plastic. When it was placed in front of the screen, it had three colours. The top third was blue, middle third a sort of beige colour and the bottom third was green. It was wonderful when you were watching a cowboy film, but not so great when people were in close-up! My grandmother who lived in the country didn't have a TV until much later when she moved to a cottage near the beach. Everyone who visited on a Saturday afternoon loved to watch the Wrestling and I also remember watching *The Beverly Hillbillies* on the black and white television she had.

We went back to school after the summer holidays, usually taking a little while to settle in to the routine again. Quite often we were asked to write about what we did on our summer holidays, and it came as no surprise that the other children's holidays were exactly the same as ours. The closest you came to a holiday was staying at your grannies house for a few days.

Autumn crept in sometimes, and other times it announced itself with blustery winds and unbelievable storms blowing around our stone farmhouse. On the way to school, we noticed trees with leaves that were different from their usual colour. We took some of the red, gold and russet leaves that were lying on the ground, into school for the nature table. Our teacher praised us for noticing God's glory. My mother and father gathered firewood to stockpile for the winter and often I would see my mother outside with a saw in her hand sawing the branches into logs or splitting the logs with an axe, working like a man while my father was at work in the town.

When we visited my father's mother in the town, we would see little birds on the telegraph wires chattering away, probably planning their journey south for the winter. Looking out her window one day, I thought it was strange seeing someone struggling with an umbrella in the wind: umbrellas weren't something we had any need for. If we had to go out in the rain, we had hoods on our duffle coats, and if we complained, my mother would say, "Run on, you are not made of sugar or salt, you will not melt." She was probably teaching us to be what the country folk called 'hardy.'

Autumn ended with Halloween, and, although it was not the American type extravaganza we know now, we looked forward to it nonetheless. It was a holiday from school, and we were ready for a break from rising early in the mornings. My mother continued to make big pots of porridge in the mornings. During the day we usually had tea, bread and jam with a bit of the fruit which my father bought from the Wednesday open air market in the town. Warming pots of stew or soup created tantalising aromas in the farmhouse kitchen during the day, as did my mother's baking. At Halloween she baked apple tarts, and she would put a silver sixpence or a silver threepenny bit with a picture of a hare on it, into them. There was great excitement as we were given a slice of it and we each hoped we would be the one to find the money.

Sometimes, she bought a couple of apple tarts from the baker who came around the countryside in his van once a week. Although they didn't taste as nice as hers, they had a gold ring in them. I wanted that ring so much and I was disappointed when my younger sister got it. Remembering a proverb I had heard at school, I said "All that glitters is not gold." OK, so I was a bad loser! I felt really sad for her when she got up the next morning and the ring was no longer gold but looked more like bronze; not only that, her finger had turned green. I wished I had not been jealous of her.

Our little Halloween party in the evening consisted of my mother's apple tarts, monkey nuts, mixed nuts, apples, and, in later years, we also got toffee apples. I don't remember us ever having fireworks, and we didn't dress up. I remember my uncle wearing a false face to look in the window one time, and I continued screaming even after he took it off. The real fun was the games we played. Apples were put in a bowl of water, and we had to keep our hands behind our back and lift the apples out using our teeth. War broke out in the kitchen when someone got their head pushed into the bowl. We called it ducking for apples, but I think the Americans call it bobbing for apples. A few apples were hung from the beam on the kitchen ceiling and again we had to take a bite out of them without holding them with our hands. They would swing to and fro — it was more difficult than it sounds. As we got a little older and were trusted with knives, we were allowed to peel an apple all in one go, holding the peel in our right hand we had to toss it over our left shoulder and if it fell in the shape of a letter of the alphabet, that was the first letter of the name of the person you would marry.

Often one of the old farmers who were our neighbours arrived, knowing my mother would have something tasty for supper. They would tease the children by telling them ghost stories. One of them told me if I sat in the dark, facing a mirror at midnight and lit a candle, the face of the man I would marry would appear in the mirror. Even though I was interested to know what he would look like I would never have sat in front of that mirror. I had everyone in the room in fits of laughter when I said, "Oh I couldn't do that, what if the devil looked out at me." I couldn't understand why they all thought it was funny.

The nights had grown dark and believe me when I say they were very dark in the country. Since there was no electricity in our area, there was only moonlight, starlight and the odd window illuminated in the neighbour's houses which were spaced far apart because it was a farming community. There was a sharp frostiness to the cold wind and once again it was winter. My mother put extra blankets on the beds and pulled the settee and chairs closer to the fire. The little stove which she called a range was always shining as she had blackened it with polish to make it look that way. A pile of logs or turf sat beside it to top up the fire every evening as it saved someone having to go out in the cold to get more when they were required.

We played board games like Ludo and Snakes and Ladders. My father taught us how to play Draughts and the old wireless supplied music or the occasional play or story in the background. My uncle brought us a Dansette record player — I think it must have worked by battery. He was a fan of Country and Western music and I remember he brought a selection of Slim Whitman, Hank Loughlin and Hank Williams records with it. My love of Country and Western music started at an early age and remains with me to this day, much to the amusement of my children.

My mother spent her evenings knitting and with a family the size of ours, there was always someone needing whatever her needles produced. In winter she would knit scarves and pixies which looked like balaclavas. I reminded my brother about them recently and he said, "Yes she used to make us wear them back to front if she wasn't pleased with us about something." Not true, but we had a good laugh about it. She would also knit mittens to keep our hands warm going to school. I remember she knitted a pair of mittens for me and because my brother didn't have any, I gave him one and told him to put his other hand in his pocket to keep it warm and I did the same. We always walked together holding hands because my mother had instructed us to do so. Meantime my mother would be knitting every chance she had so my brother's mittens would be ready for the next morning.

The trees looked different in winter: they had

bare branches and the coloured leaves had all gone. Most of the children walked to school, their cheeks rosy because of the cold, and their warm breath was like little clouds in the frosty air. We walked on the snow-covered grass verges because the icy roads were hazardous. When we got to school, there were little bottles of milk warming beside the pot-bellied stove for us, though we had to wait until break time for them. When the snow came, flowers disappeared, there were fewer birds around and the teacher told us about the little animals going into hibernation. At the time I wished children could do the same. I suppose it wasn't all bad, we were able to build snowmen. At school we began counting the days until the Birthday of the Christ Child. We could hardly wait for Jesus' birthday and the Christmas holidays.

Decorating the Christmas tree was one of my favourite things. My father brought a fir tree into the house after he had planted it in a bucket of sand. We made paper chains for it. Little silver tinfoil bun cases and squashed milk bottle tops were threaded and hung on it with a few precious glass baubles. Tinsel added a bit of glitter, and it would not have been complete without a few blown up balloons, (which were starting to deflate by the next morning.) We thought it was the most beautiful tree ever, despite the fact there were no lights on it. What you never had you never miss.

Paper streamers went from one corner of the ceiling to its diagonal opposite, the same being done with the other two corners until it formed a colourful X at ceiling height. Holly was brought in to adorn the tops of any pictures we had on the walls. With the stuffed turkey or goose cooking in the oven, a pot of chicken broth on top of the stove and my grandmother's plum duff (Christmas Pudding) sitting on the table, it was beginning to smell a lot like Christmas. My mother always prepared everything on Christmas Eve as she would never have managed to do it all on Christmas morning. With a row of little stockings hung on the rack above the stove and a mince pie and ginger wine left on the table for Santa, we were an excited little family of children and I think it was nearly midnight before we were all asleep.

When people tell you what they got in their stockings as children, they are not lying. There was a silver sixpence, a mandarin orange and a selection box of sweets and chocolate and one main present. The girls in our house got a doll each and the boys got a cowboy outfit or cap guns with a belt and holsters. Sometimes we got something to wear. We could not have been happier. Santa Claus had been very good to us, and it meant we had been well behaved children throughout the year. His approval meant everything to us. After Christmas we settled down for the long winter ahead. It seemed as if the Earth had gone to sleep until it was Spring once more.

Energy Awareness

I thought back through my life to a time when I was a child of about nine years old. We were living on the farm and my paternal grandmother was staying with us for the night. She came to look after us if my mother had an appointment with the doctor or when it was time for making hay. She looked after the younger children and made food for everyone while my mother worked outside. In the evening, my mother, grandmother and I were sitting around the stove in the farmhouse kitchen. I was feeling very grown up, being allowed to stay up late when the other children went to bed. The two women were talking about my grandfather who had passed away before I was born. Suddenly I got this strange feeling like pins and needles all over my body. I told them how I was feeling, and my mother said, "Oh, someone has walked over your grave." She had to explain to me that it was just something people in Ireland said to explain the feeling. I realise now that I must have been sensing his Spirit with us.

When I went to bed at night, I had a certain dread

of an old wardrobe in the corner of the room. I had trouble getting to sleep and I would make up stories to amuse myself while I lay there only glancing at the wardrobe every now and then. Sometimes I was more afraid than others and I would pull the sheet over my head. I suppose that would be considered playing dead nowadays. I never told my mother or anyone else of my fear; I was worried they would think I was being silly. After all, my mother opened the wardrobe and brought clothes out or hung clothes in it on a daily basis, and I could not see anything unusual in it then. Perhaps the firelight and the shadows from the flickering oil lamp in the bedroom at night created the spooky atmosphere, I don't know.

Living in Ireland, people visited each other's houses in the evenings at a time when there was no electricity, never mind television. It gave the farmers a chance to compare notes on the prices of livestock and talk about farming in general. There was a man called Johnny who lived in a house at the end of our country lane who told my mother he would come to our house in the fore supper. Well, I told my mother I thought he was very cheeky inviting himself for supper. She laughed and told me that meant he was coming before supper, not for supper! However, tea and the best food in the house were produced for anyone who came to visit, as was customary with all the neighbours.

I loved it when a few people gathered in our house for the evening. I was what you would call a curious child. Sometimes my mother would say "Run on to bed now — you will not miss anything." However, I loved to hear the stories they told. It was ok when they talked of local happenings and passed on whatever gossip they had heard, but invariably the talk often turned to Ghost Stories and Banshees. In Ireland, the Banshee is seen as the spirit of a wailing woman, who is the harbinger of bad news. The men insisted these stories were absolutely true; they always knew someone these things had happened to. I used to be afraid to go to the outside toilet after those stories. I had once asked my grandmother if there was any such thing as ghosts. I think her answer must have comforted me at the time. She said, "There is no such thing as ghosts. If you die and go to Heaven, you won't want to come back and if you die and go to Hell, the devil won't let you come back." She believed our spirits go to Heaven or Hell, but she had no time for any talk about ghosts. It was such a relief to my worried little mind to hear her say that.

I really knew what fear was one time. Our lane was a quarter of a mile long and I set off to walk to school. I must have been about eight years old then, and my mother had cut my hair. It was the first time it had been cut since I was born, whether she was tired of the morning struggles of detangling it, I don't know. Anyway, she had cut it into a short bob style. The sun was behind me that morning and I could see my shadow ahead of me as I walked. My head looked like a mushroom! I was thinking I didn't like my shadow when something at the old derelict house before the end of the lane claimed my attention. A strange man with a bald head was bent over a piece of machinery. He hadn't noticed me because whatever he was working with was making a noise. I walked backwards for a few steps and then I turned and ran up the lane as fast as my legs would carry me.

By the time I arrived at the house, I was crying, and it took a little while before I could tell my mother there was a man at the end of the lane with a bomb and I couldn't pass him to go to school. My mother told me I was talking a lot of nonsense, but she picked the baby up in her arms and set off down the lane with me. Why were my brothers not with me? It must have been at one of those rare times when they had mumps or measles. When we got to the end of the lane, the man was still there. My mother began laughing, "Oh for goodness sake, it is only Johnny with the cement mixer," she said. Now, Johnny was the neighbour who visited our house at least once a fortnight. How could I not have known him? Well, I had never seen him without his cap, and when he was bent over working, I didn't see his face, only the top of his bald head. As for thinking he had a bomb, I had never seen a cement mixer in my life. My father mixed cement with a shovel. Needless to say, I was late when I arrived at school that day. I don't remember what excuse I gave but it couldn't have been the truth as I don't remember being made to feel shame at my foolishness.

I suppose you could say I had a wonderful childhood, one that children who live in the town would never experience. I had gained a love of nature — flowers, animals, birds and insects. Well, maybe not earwigs! If you were to ask me if I was psychic at that age, I wouldn't have had a clue what you meant. I certainly had a few strange feelings and occasionally if I met someone I didn't know, I would keep a good distance away from them. Maybe all children feel like that, I don't know.

I remember one time my grandmother's sister was visiting, and after she had tea, I was taking her cup to the basin to be washed. The tea had been made in the old-fashioned way with leaves, and, as I looked into her cup, the tea leaves seemed to form the map of Australia. I asked her if she was planning to go to Australia, and she laughed. She didn't answer me, but she said to my mother, "Well as sure as goodness, your mother will never be dead while that one is alive." I didn't know what she meant at the time but I suppose she thought I was able to tell what would happen in the future, just like my grandmother. She didn't go to Australia, but her son was on his way home from there at the time, for a surprise visit.

Did God feature in my life as a child? Of course, He did. I do not think there was a time when God was not in my life. Although we were not regular churchgoers, we said our prayers on a daily basis. God was the person I talked to when I was afraid, and, as an adult, I still talk to Him at those times when I find life difficult. I have also learned to thank Him and not to make requests all the time. These days I ask for Healing and Blessings for others, and He may not answer immediately, but I know He will in His own time and in His own way. What did I think God was like then? I thought of Him as the benevolent father, someone who loved me like my daddy did, only more. He loved all of His children on the whole Earth. He loved all of us the same, whether our skin was white, black, brown, or yellow; it made no difference to Him. Through our teachings at school, I knew of the different colours of the people on the Earth, but also because my mother didn't like us being wasteful with our food. We were told how children in other countries were starving and it was sinful if we left food on our plates at the end of a meal.

When I was ten, my parents decided to sell the farm, and we moved to the town with all its conveniences. The indoor flush toilet was wonderful and my mother loved the twin tub washing machine because it washed and spun the clothes almost dry before they were hung on the clothes line. It made her life so much easier, but electricity and television brought a different lifestyle. Sometimes, it would have been nice to be back in the evenings of storytelling in front of the stove in our farmhouse kitchen in the country. I could imagine the light from the Tilly lamp with the faint smell of paraffin oil pervading the air. The rattle of cups as my mother made a final cup of tea before bed, a signal to the visiting farmers that afterwards it would be time to go home. It was the end of an era that had held local characters, laughter and friendship and I missed all of it.

A Time of Change

While we were living at the new house, a couple of things happened to rock my world. As I have said before, my father always wanted a better life for us and when he saw a chance to immigrate to Australia under the Assisted Passage Scheme, he and my mother discussed it and decided we should go. On our arrival we would be met by a minister and his wife, they would sponsor us until my father found work. During the time my father worked in the furniture shop, he had become quite an expert at fitting carpets and laying flooring; he knew his services would be in demand, and he could put his skills to good use. Besides, he was not afraid of hard work, and he was prepared to do everything he could to make the new venture a success. Our new life in the sun was on the horizon, and, for a while, it filled our dreams as well as every waking moment. They say all good things come to an end, and so it was with us. At the last minute, my mother decided she just could not go to Australia, and that was the end of that. She wasn't prepared to leave her mother, mother-in-law and all that was familiar to her. No Kangaroos or Koalas for us, after all. Despite the fact we had all passed our medical and the luggage labels had arrived for any of our belongings that had to be transported by boat, we were to remain in Northern Ireland. I wasn't very disappointed as it was outside of my control. Later we would watch Skippy the Bush Kangaroo on television and imagine what we had missed.

What happened next was something that should have been within my grasp. While attending my old school I had been about to sit my 11 plus examination which was a selection process for Grammar School. After the move to the new school I sat my exam. What can I say? I failed, and I had only myself to blame. Maybe if I had been happy at the new school, it might have made a difference, I don't know. After having the gentle headmistress at my previous school, I found the new headmaster extremely strict and watching him administer punishment by slapping children with a ruler didn't sit well with my sensitive nature. Getting into the Grammar School had meant a lot to me and now it would not be happening. After the initial disappointment and tears on the day of the results, I knew my parents and I had to make new plans. It helped that all of the children, except one, from my Primary school class would be going to the same secondary school as me, and when you are eleven, that means a lot to you. I wouldn't say I enjoyed my time at the Secondary School but I was always in the top class for my year and I did the best I could while I was there.

A couple of years later, a small farm came onto the market, and my father, being a farmer at heart, decided to buy it. We moved into the house, which was not as remote as the previous one from my early childhood. In fact, it was only a couple of miles from my grandmother, who had left her little cottage in the Sallagh Braes and moved nearer to the sea after a hard winter. She and my uncle shared a cottage which was bigger than her last one. Now she had two bedrooms, one on the ground floor and one upstairs. There was a large living room, and she created a little kitchen area under the stairs. In place of the stove, she now had a gas cooker, and, in the living room, a tiled Devon fireplace. It was nice as an open fire but no use for cooking on. Around the fireplace she displayed her brass ornaments, plates and kettles. They shone in the firelight, and I think my uncle cleaned them weekly with Brasso. He would spread newspapers on the kitchen table before he proceeded with his task, which was quite messy but produced wonderful results.

The only noticeable difference in my grandmother's bedroom, apart from the fact that it was bigger than the last one, was the pelmets above the curtains. They were made from wood and painted cream. Displayed on top of them was a row of Toby Jugs. I could never see them as beautiful; they looked like little men with ugly faces, but at least they were up high and only the colours were obvious at first glance.

There were a few other houses in the little area near her cottage; I think they were owned by her family. My great grandmother lived in one of the houses with my grandmother's sister. My grandmother's brother and his wife lived in another. It may sound like an ideal arrangement, but I don't know that my grandmother was entirely happy with it. You see, she felt the others knew too much of her business at times, or at least I felt that is how my grandmother saw it. Sometimes the adults would raise their voices when visiting and I would go outside. I remember playing in the little street and fetching buckets of water from the cow tail pump when she needed them, usually spilling a lot of it by the time I got back to her house.

My grandmother kept her cottage as spic and span as she had the one in the Sallagh Braes. It was homely and comfortable. She was a woman who made the most of what life gave her. Although she had done everything she could with her new home, I got the feeling she yearned for the little cottage in the Sallagh Braes sometimes. Her lovely blue eyes had a faraway look now and again and I knew not to talk and interrupt her thoughts. There were times when her new cottage was filled with her laughter as well, so looking back I think with the milder winters, she made the right move.

I have always thought of Ireland as being a land of superstitions. Listening to the conversations as a child when the old farmers were visiting must have had an effect on me! I didn't know that I would soon find out about a superstition that was associated with some of the families in Ireland.

My grandmother's cottage was somewhere I loved to visit. There was a cosiness and warmth that had nothing to do with her open fire. I now know that it was her loving energy that radiated throughout her home even when the fire was not lit. One evening after seeking permission from my mother I walked the two miles to her house. We sat together and talked for a little while and realising I had to be home before it got dark I said goodbye to her and left. I hadn't gone very far when I turned back; I had forgotten to give my grandmother a kiss! I explained why I had returned and when I gave her a kiss she laughed and said, "That is two you have given me this evening."

Later that night I was in bed when I called to my mother, "There is a knock at the door." She checked and assured me there wasn't anyone there. I heard the knocking again and the same thing happened. I thought it was strange as I was sure I had heard the loud knocks. Next morning, I was awakened by a knock on the door and when my mother answered it; my uncle's boss was standing there. My uncle had gone to check on my grandmother when she hadn't called him to get up to go to work as she usually did. He found she had passed away in her sleep. At that moment my uncle's boss had arrived to take him to work and my uncle sent him to give the sad news to my mother.

When I heard what had happened, I locked myself in the little outside toilet and cried. I would never see my lovely grandmother again. I was glad I had gone back the night before to give her a kiss. Later my mother told me that the knocks I had heard follow some families as a sign of death. This was not something we discussed before or after that day, and, at the time, I hoped I would never hear them again. What puzzled me, though, was that no one else in the house heard them that night.

The time my grandmother passed was the first time I had seen my father cry. She had been good to my mother and father. Although my father was close to his own mother, he also loved my mother's mother. They shared the same sense of humour and many a good laugh they had together. For me, and perhaps some of my siblings, it was a time that showed us the great loss we feel when someone dies. We were in no doubt that my grandmother's soul would have gone to Heaven. She believed in God and she had been good to everyone she met. Years later, people would tell me how kind my grandmother had been to them, making sure they had something to eat when times were hard. For a long time, our home was a place of sadness. Thankfully people are right when they say time is a great healer. Our loved ones, who have passed, remain in our hearts but eventually life takes over again for us. There is no time limit for grief, but we can't change what has happened and we have to get on and do the best we can. The Christian belief that we shall see our loved ones again when we leave the Earth was a great comfort to us at the time.

Going to America

After about a year we sold the farm and moved back to the town where the family remained for the next six years. Well, most of them did! My father's brother came home from America for a holiday and after much discussion it was decided that my family would immigrate. My mother being cautious after our failed attempt at immigrating to Australia decided that my father, brother and I should go to America first, get settled and then she and the other five children would join us. We travelled to America but within a short time my father became so homesick that he and my brother returned to Northern Ireland and I stayed there with my uncle and aunt for six months. I have often wondered if things would have been different if my mother and the rest of the family had gone with us. I honestly feel that my father could have settled if my mother had been with him. He came from a big family, had a big family of seven children and to him family was the most important thing in his life. I think without my mother and his children around him he felt bereft.

We had arrived in America in the month of March, so I attended school for three months and had a wonderful summer holiday for three months. I returned home, but during that time my outlook on life had changed. There was a whole big world out there to explore! The next few years were hard because I was a young teenager and freedom and travel were not available to me. I kept thinking there was more to life than this. I couldn't wait to grow up, but I attended school for the next two years and left at the age of fifteen to look after the family while my mother worked. Boyfriends came along, but my curfew times were too early for me. When we went to the pictures — or cinema, as it is known today — I had to leave before the end of the film to be home before 9.45 pm. Whether it was because I was the eldest of seven or the fact that I had been separated from the family for so long, I felt my father was trying his best to protect me. I left school, aged fifteen, and looked after my brothers and sisters for a year to enable my mother to go out to work. Then I realised I was missing out on a lot by not working like other girls my age. They seemed carefree and happy, and they were having so much fun. I talked to my parents about it, and they agreed that I could look for work. Very soon I found a job in a large department store. Initially I worked on the cosmetics counter, but eventually a position became available in the office and I was chosen for the position because I'd had experience of book keeping and typing in my last two years at school.

Meeting the Love of My Life

During my lunch break in the store one day, I noticed a couple of good looking young men. Daniel was as dark haired as his friend David was fair. We got talking and I discovered they worked with my uncle in the local factory. They started visiting the store every weekday at lunch time and I realised I was falling in love with one of them. I couldn't understand why he didn't ask me out on a date. What was wrong with me? I wasn't bad looking and I had a reasonably good figure. My long brown hair hung down to my waist and shone from all the brushing I gave it — a neighbour had once told me it was my crowning glory. With the confidence of youth, I felt I would have made a suitable girlfriend for him. After a few months, my uncle said, "You know the two boys who work with me, one of them would like to take you out for lunch." Smiling, I asked if it was the dark haired one. I couldn't believe it when he said, "No, it is the fair haired one." I told him I was sorry, but I was hoping it was the other one. The fair haired one stopped coming in to see me but the dark haired one continued to come alone. He still didn't ask me out though.

One day he came in as usual, his blue eyes scanning the store for me. When he found me and walked towards me, I said "I am busy; I don't have time to talk today." Just as I was walking away, he said, "That is a pity because I was going to ask you to go to a Dance at the weekend." I accepted his invitation, but we had to go to a local Dance instead of the one he had in mind which was thirty miles away. I felt such a fool saying my parents wouldn't allow me to go that far, and anyway, I would have to be home early. I was sixteen, and he was four years older than me, so I suppose my parents were protecting me. I didn't see it that way at the time. We went out together on the Saturday evening, and he was everything I had hoped he would be — kind, considerate and smartly dressed. During the evening he explained he had wanted to take me out for ages, but he was building a car. He was an engineer and, although he had borrowed his father's car that night, he was fiercely independent and wanted to have his Mini on the road before we started dating. I should have been on top of the world, but he also told me he was going to sea on board an oil tanker for four and a half months soon, working as a junior engineer. By the time he was ready to go to sea I was so much in love with him, I would have promised to wait for him forever.

At sixteen I felt restricted by the rules at home, and I thought it was time for a change. I moved into a bedsit with two of the girls from work. Basically it was one massive room with three single beds as well as couches, tables etc. We had the use of the shared bathroom and kitchen. It was an old house but it had an upbeat vibe. On the first night we were lying in our beds in our shared room and after the lights had been turned off it was very dark. I lay quietly for a few minutes to make sure I wasn't imagining things and then suddenly I said, "I feel as if there is someone else here, I can sense their breathing." The others shouted, "Shut up" in unison and after that I learned to keep quiet as it was obvious others could not sense some of the things that I could. Had my sixth sense kicked in way back then?

When I left home at sixteen, I felt that I was in a position to change my life. I was earning my own money and could make my own decisions. While I thought I had changed a little, my parents thought I had changed a lot. When I moved into the bedsit with the other girls, we found ourselves sharing a kitchen and bathroom with the people in the bedsit across the hall. It so happened they were two Mormon Elders, which meant they belonged to the Church of Jesus Christ of Latter Day Saints. They were good boys with good principles. I started going to Church with them and I enjoyed the services they had there. I practiced what they preached. No smoking, no drinking, no sex before marriage and no tea or coffee. Looking back, I believe this was a way of life that meant I looked after myself at a vulnerable age.

My parents weren't pleased about me going to the Mormon Church. My mother told me that she and my father wanted to meet these boys. Even though I was no longer living at home my parents still had a big influence on my life. I invited them home and my father wasn't a bit interested in them, but my mother tried to give them tea despite the fact I had warned her that they didn't drink tea or coffee. Immaculately dressed in their suits, shirts and ties my mother couldn't fail to be impressed by these handsome American Elders. They had impeccable manners and were very respectful at all times. On reflection, I suppose I enjoyed being in their company because they reminded me of the American boys I had gone to school with. It turned out to be more of a social evening than anything else. At least my mother wasn't threatening to bring the minister in to talk to me as she had before. After their visit I continued to go to their church and my mother said no more about it. Meeting them must have convinced her that their intentions were honourable. I asked her what she thought of them and all she said was that she couldn't see what harm a cup of tea would have done them.

Getting Married and Going to Sea

My boyfriend Daniel returned from sea and I realised that my feelings for him hadn't changed. He was extremely good looking in a similar way to George Best, the Manchester United footballer who came from Belfast. His eyes were even bluer than I remembered because of the suntan he had acquired. He spent his time on leave taking me to visit his family, my family and married friends we had made before he had gone to sea. All too soon it was time for him to go away again. My heart was broken but we wrote to each other on a regular basis. This pattern continued for a while, but I missed him each time he went away.

My mother had been really upset when I left to join the other girls in the bedsit, and she coaxed me into returning home. I felt I had put her through so much that I gave in and moved back to live with the family again. Shortly after that Daniel returned from a trip to sea and asked me to marry him. It was decided we would get married the day after my eighteenth birthday. Daniel was twenty-two. He proposed privately and we sealed our engagement with a beautiful sapphire and diamond ring which we chose together a few days later. My parents did not have much warning that they would have to pay for our grand wedding with a reception in Ballygally Castle. They didn't complain about it, and the wedding was arranged for about six weeks from the date of the proposal. I was a very proud girl when I walked up the aisle of the church on my father's arm, seeing the man I loved dressed in his Merchant Navy uniform patiently awaiting my arrival. He looked so handsome and when he looked at me with love in his eyes, I knew I was doing the right thing. The nerves I had felt that morning left me. We had decided we would get married in the church he attended, which was Presbyterian.

I didn't attend the Mormon Church again, as I was going to sea with my husband soon after the wedding. I still appreciate the fact that I was looked after during the time I did go to the church, though. I didn't realise it then, but I think that was the beginning of my Spiritual journey. I began to understand that there were other religions and not just the one I had been brought up in, and all of those religions thought they were right in their beliefs. After our wedding we had our honeymoon in the Isle of Man. Soon we would be travelling together to the Persian

Gulf on an oil tanker; hence the rush to get married before his leave was over.

It was by going to sea with my husband that I had what I now think of as a spiritual awakening. Usually there would have been four or five wives travelling on board ship with their husbands. On this occasion, I was the only woman on board for a month, the others having gone home. In the afternoons I would walk around the deck of the oil tanker for exercise. I would go up to the bow of the ship and sit amongst the ropes for a little while and look at the sea. Sometimes, to my delight, I would see porpoises playing as the effervescence sparkled on top of the waves in the afternoon sunlight. Often there would be flying fish leaping above the water as a magnificent shoal. One day while sitting alone, staring at the sea, something spoke to my Soul. I realised that I had peace and beauty all around me and I knew it had been created by someone. I also knew without doubt that whoever created all of that peace and beauty also created me. I had a sense of being part of it but also being the observer of it all. I realised we are all connected to each other and to every single thing upon the Earth. I was young at that time, not yet nineteen years old. My mind only took in the Earth we live upon; it was much later in my life that I thought about the connection to the Universe and the Universes beyond ours.

Now, in my mind's eye, I imagine the golden threads joining everything. In other words, we are all one, dependent upon each other and all things. Although we share the Earth, it does not have infinite resources. We have a responsibility to it and to the other Planets for the wellbeing of our solar system. Everything depends on balance and that is why I say we depend upon each other and upon all things. In the 1960s, meteorologist Edward Lorenz used the term 'The Butterfly Effect' to describe how small changes can have a big impact on the weather conditions in other countries. I think the quote was, 'A butterfly can flap its wings in Peking and in Central Park you get rain instead of sunshine.' There is some debate as to whether this is right; I am neither a scientist nor a meteorologist, but I think there is something in the overall theory.

I saw the ultimate creator of everything as God. I had believed in Him all my life. I have said I was still a teenager then, and yes, I did think of God as the old white haired man with a long beard sitting on His throne overseeing everything, Angels everywhere doing His bidding. I didn't talk to anyone about those feelings I had on the ship — it was between God and me. It was a strange feeling that day and it made me want to write poetry or something. I didn't, but I wish now that I had; it would have been lovely to look back on.

We had got married when I was eighteen, and I was conscious of the fact that some people might have thought I was pregnant, the wedding had been arranged so hastily. However, that was not the case: we had to be married during Daniel's leave so that I could travel with him. It was the 1970s and people got married young then. We had a honeymoon in the Isle of Man and when we returned, we rented a cottage from his grandmother. Daniel was an engineer for a well-known oil tanker company, and I had just had a four and a half month trip to sea with him. It was not my intention to travel with him every time. On my return, I found a job in a shoe shop. You could say I was a people person, and I loved working in retail. There was also the fact that, although my married life had just begun, I wasn't quite ready to give up my independence. There was only one problem with my new job — the money was poor, especially when I heard how much friends were earning in a local factory that made components for telephones and televisions. I decided I would apply for a job there, and after an interview, I was given a date to start work.

My parents were both working in the factory by then, and my father came to see me at break time. "How are you getting on?" he asked. "I don't like it dad. I might as well be a battery hen. A conveyer belt passes by, and I install so many parts in this thing and then I do the same over and over again." He laughed, but I didn't. I told him I was not going to stay. You couldn't even see God's daylight, as there were no windows in the place. He became serious. "Think of the money. Give it a chance. You can't leave, as I have spoken to the bosses for you to get you the job" he said. Well, I tried until lunch time and when I saw him again I said, "I have to go, dad, this place would put my head away (which meant if I stayed any longer I would end up with mental health issues.) Looking around me, I saw so many people doing the same job. They were happy, laughing, chatting as they worked. I felt guilty that I could not be more like them, grateful to have a job, especially one that paid so well. The truth was I felt as if I had tried and failed to have the common sense to know when I was well off. At that point in time, I just needed to get out of there, so I asked my father if he remembered what it was like for him in America. My father looked at me with a stern look on his face, then, his face softening, he told me I needed to get a pass from the foreman to get out the gate. The place felt even more like a prison. I picked up my handbag and coat and walked out the door. At the gate I was met by a security man who was built like a tank. He demanded my pass. I pushed past him saying, "I need no pass." He probably noticed that I was on the verge of tears and let me go.

I walked and walked. It was snowing by then, and I began running, holding my face up, enjoying the feeling of the snowflakes falling on it. I didn't even care that I was getting wet; it was good to taste freedom again. It felt so good to be out in the fresh air that it came as a shock when I realised I must have walked two miles and had another two to go before I got home. Someone I knew stopped their car and offered me a lift home, which I gladly accepted. When I got home I took off my wet clothes and got into bed, had a good sleep and later when I was feeling rested I phoned my old boss in the shoe shop and told him I didn't like the new job. Well, he had said I was to let him know how I got on. He told me to come back to work on Monday and he would give me an extra couple of pounds per week. I was happy, but the story of my foray into factory work didn't end there. I got a letter telling me to come back and collect my wages for the morning I had worked. I was worried they might try to talk me into coming back to work there, and I never did go back for my wages. Needless to say, my mother and father weren't too happy about how I had let them down at the time, but after a while they saw the funny side of it, and they reminded me occasionally of the half day I had worked on the TV line.

After I returned to the shoe shop, I was very grateful that my boss had taken me back. I was happy going to work in the mornings and I told my father that money wasn't everything. "No, but it is very handy to go to the shops with," he replied. Eventually I left the shoe shop, as I felt it was time for another trip to sea with Daniel. After the voyage we returned home, and I decided I wanted to settle down and start a family. Thankfully Daniel agreed with me. Life on the ship had been wonderful, but for me it was a false existence with no older people or children on board.

Becoming a Little Family

I knew I would be lonely while Daniel was away, so I got a job in a D.I.Y. shop. It was a hardware shop selling everything connected with home improvement but on a smaller scale than a Builders Merchant. It was the early 1970s, a time when work was plentiful. The shop was privately owned — this was long before the big D.I.Y. stores came to Northern Ireland — and was the kind of shop where you needed to be quite knowledgeable about the merchandise. Customers came into the shop and expected you to plan the projects they had in mind, never mind sell them whatever they needed!

I loved the work and took great satisfaction from it. I learned so much and was able to discuss things with my engineer husband when he was on leave. Things I had not known anything about before. I thought I knew everything, and he didn't always agree with me. However, it brought a new dimension to our relationship; life was more interesting at dinnertime. Daniel didn't realise that I bowed to his superior knowledge and learned a lot during our conversations.

The job in the DIY shop came at just the right time for me because we had bought a brand new bungalow in a nearby town. I got a discount on everything we needed, floor tiles and paint etc. During the time I was working there I found out I was expecting my first baby. I decided I would have to leave work because not only was I no longer able to lift anything heavy, but I had the most awful morning sickness. I was so ill I had to have a bucket in the car when I was travelling to work in the mornings. You would have thought that experience would have been enough to put me off having any more children, but our little son was such a joy to both of us. After his arrival there was no question of me leaving him with someone else while I went out to work in retail? I know that some mothers would love to have the opportunity to stay at home and bring up their babies, but it didn't come without some sacrifices. We had enough money to pay the bills but not too much left over. I didn't mind that. I knew I wanted a home for my son where at least one parent was there all the time and luckily Daniel agreed. My new little son, Alan, was dependant on me and I loved our time together. I had a new home, a car, my baby son and a little dog, and, despite the fact Daniel was away most of the time, my life was pretty complete. I was happy.

One and a half years later I discovered I was expecting another baby and thankfully the pregnancy was going like a dream. I felt healthy and well and didn't have morning sickness. I felt so well, in fact, that we sold the bungalow and wasted no time in buying the old stone cottage that had belonged to Daniel's grandmother. It was a renovation project but that didn't deter us. During the time of the renovations, we moved into a caravan on the site. Just when I thought Daniel and I would not fit in the double sleeping bag for much longer, the house became habitable. We moved in, and a second little baby son was born. We called him Gary. He was just a few weeks old when Daniel returned to Sea. The house had a lovely atmosphere, as it had belonged to my husband's grandmother, who had passed away. I didn't have any concerns about Daniel going to sea and leaving me there with the two boys. After all, his brother lived next door and his mother lived further up the lane. What could go wrong?

Not long after Daniel went away to Sea, things changed. I could hear noises during the night. I tried to convince myself it was the house cooling down when the floorboards were creaking. One night, it unnerved me so much that I took the riding crop and went downstairs to investigate. I didn't find anything! I also had the feeling that there had once been a stone staircase on the outside wall of the house.

Sometimes I would hear a creak in the corner of my bedroom and imagine a door opening into the room. I watched the corner just as I had the old wardrobe when I was a little girl. I talked to my mother-in-law about my feeling that it might have had stone stairs on the outside of the gable wall at one time. She didn't remember them being there but said it was quite possible as it was common for this to be the case on farms. She also told me there had been a mill in the area, but it was long before she was born and she wasn't sure of its exact location. I told myself I was missing my husband Daniel and my imagination was working overtime. I knew I had to get used to being on my own with the boys.

Being alone with two small children, I didn't attend church very often. I still had great faith in God, though. When our first son, Alan, was born, the question of having him christened came up. We decided we would have him christened in the Presbyterian Church. Daniel was Presbyterian, as were his forefathers, and it seemed like the right thing to do. Our second son, Gary, had arrived two years later, and we had him baptised in the same way. For most of my married life, I didn't give much thought to how I felt spiritually: I believed in God and brought my two sons up in much the same way I had been brought up, teaching them their prayers and listening to them at bedtime while they repeated them as my mother had done with me and my siblings. However, I didn't bring out the Bible to have oaths sworn on it. I decided I would leave that for people who were attending court. When they were old enough our sons went to Sunday School and Bible Class for a short time. At the age of eleven, they no longer wanted to go, and since I hadn't liked being told what to do as far as religion was concerned when I was younger, I let them decide for themselves. At least I had armed them with some knowledge in the beliefs of Christianity. I wanted more than anything for them to grow up to be decent human beings.

What can I say; life took over during those years. My husband was at sea for twelve years, working four and a half months away and usually spending two months at home afterwards. Looking back on those early years is difficult for me; I was lonely despite being busy bringing up our boys.

After our second little boy was born, my mother and father separated — it was just before their twenty-fifth wedding anniversary. My mother had married young, and she had a big family to care for as well as the farm in the early years of her marriage. I honestly don't think she ever stopped loving my father; I suppose she felt she needed a break from all the hard work once the children were grown up. She saw the chance of a new life and took it. Like the rest of us, my father was devastated when she left, but, in time, he came to terms with it. She went to England and later to the Isle of Man, and, of course, we all visited her as much as we could. It was the perfect place for me to take the boys for holidays while Daniel was away, and she was always happy to see us. It was during one of those holidays that something happened I will never forget.

Visiting Fortune Tellers

As a young woman, I had been to see a handful of people known as fortune tellers. In the beginning, I went to find out if there was a tall dark handsome stranger in my future. I was fascinated by some of the information I was given, and, if I am honest, I was curious as to how a complete stranger could give me accurate details about my life.

Only a couple of those visits were memorable. The first was to a lady called Gypsy Rose Lee. She told me I would always remember going to see her. Some of the things she told me sounded improbable. She said I would work with lots of children, and I didn't have any desire to: I felt that by helping my mother with my younger siblings I had played my part in rearing children, and, although I enjoyed bringing up my own boys, I had no plans for working with children! She was right, however; in the future, I became a tour guide showing hundreds of children around a castle. She also told me I might work in the hospitality industry, as she saw me working with china cups, plates, cutlery and glasses.

Eventually I did work in a gift shop where the owners prided themselves on being purveyors of fine china and glass. While selling all of the items she mentioned, I remembered her words. Later in my life, I found myself providing bed and breakfast accommodation for tourists and her words came back to me again.

On another occasion I visited my mother, who was living on the Isle of Man, and she told me she had heard of a witch who was very good at telling people what would happen in their future. I had never been to a witch before, and, although I was a bit nervous, I asked my mother if she would make an appointment for the two of us. Whether she was comfortable with the idea of joining me, I will never know, but I think she may have agreed to accompany me just to please me. On the evening of the appointment, we got dressed up with great excitement, wondering if this lady was as good as people said she was at knowing what the future held.

Just as we were about to leave, someone called at the house and delayed our departure. I hate being late for anything, and I told my mother so. My stepfather, who had been quietly listening, said, "I don't know what you are worrying about, if this woman is as good as they say, she will know that you are going to be late." He laughed heartily at his own wit. We had quite a walk to the alleyway where she lived, and my mother nudged me when we reached the little whitewashed, terraced cottage. While we were waiting for the door to be answered, she noticed the window dressing of tiny witches, cats and moons. The door swung open, and we went inside to see quite a normal looking woman; her nose and chin did not meet as I had expected. Where was the black cat and broomstick as in the stories of old? The lady was dark-haired, dark-eyed, a little bohemian in her dress and warm and welcoming.

There was a shiny brass figure of a man on the wall, and my mum, looking fearful, whispered to me, "That's the devil." Seeing where our attention had gone the lady said, "That's the Boss." While I didn't think he looked like the devil, I wasn't comforted by her answer, and there was a little fear in my stomach. She took us over to her kitchen table in turn and some of the things she said were true. I overheard her saying to my mother that she had had a past life as an opera singer. I don't remember a lot about what she told me, but I do remember she said I was a mountaineer in Switzerland in a past life. She asked me if I was afraid of heights and when I said no, she told me I hadn't met my death mountaineering. We paid our money and left her, feeling happy with all she had said to us.

When we got out into the street, my mum and I

laughed the whole way home. Linking my arm affectionately through hers, I said to her, "you were never an opera singer; sure everyone says you are the spitting image of Dolly Parton." Quick as a flash, she told me I had never been a mountaineer, "sure you fell off the two steps when you were cleaning the windows." It had been a bit of fun to us, and we hadn't taken it too seriously. My mum passed away seven years ago, God Bless her Soul. She passed peacefully after having pneumonia: she had been confined to her chair for years with the pain of arthritis, and it was a blessing when she was taken away from all her pain. It was a few months before my sixtieth birthday, and I miss her terribly. We had one thing in common — we loved telling a good story. The story of our visit to the witch was repeated many times over the years. We laughed about it together often.

I thought of all the experiences I'd had over the years, and I wondered if they meant I was psychic. Until the day I met the Healer, I suppose you could have dismissed them as the overactive imagination of a child, a young girl, a young woman. Meeting the man in Spain, who was a Medium, with his many gifts, including clairvoyance and healing, hearing all of the things he was able to tell me about my grandmother, mother and incidents from my childhood proved to me that there is life after death. I felt that my grandmother must have been communicating with him; after all, she was the only one who knew of my past. I didn't have any other explanation for the things he knew. I wondered if I was to become a healer like him would my intuition allow me to know the secrets of others. Would I be given messages from people who had left the Earth to pass on to their loved ones the way he seemed to be able to do?

I thought long and hard about the changes I would have to make in my life after being told I was a healer. Did this mean I would have to go to Church all the time? I had been brought up a Unitarian, a non-subscribing Presbyterian — whatever that means. My family weren't regular attenders; we went sometimes. We had been taught to say our prayers as soon as we could talk; and my mother heard our prayers every night. We said 'The Lord's Prayer' and asked God to bless everyone in our family by name. We also said a little prayer which went like this:

There are four Corners on my bed,
There are four Angels spread around,
If I should die before I wake,
I hope the Lord my Soul shall take.

I never forgot that prayer, and I continued to say it over the years. It has brought me great comfort to think there are Angels watching over us as we sleep. To me, communication with God has been a private thing; I have never felt that I needed anyone to intervene on my behalf asking for forgiveness for me. God has never been a stranger to me, and I hope He has never felt that I am a stranger to Him. I had never been the type of person to push my religion on to others. I have always felt that we are guided from above when we ask for help, or when the time is right for us. A friend told me I could not be a Christian if I did not try to bring others to God: I have never professed myself to be a Christian for that reason. I also knew that if I professed to be a Christian, I would never be able to withstand the way others would judge me. Had I taken the easy way out? Perhaps, but I never wanted to be described as a Holy Joe, Holy Roller or Bible Thumper. I knew I would continue to worship God in my own quiet way, but if the occasion arose, I would attend a church of any denomination knowing that the people there were seeking that still small voice within themselves. Whether consciously or unconsciously, I feel we would all like to know the meaning of life on Earth.

My mind travelled back to holidays with my mother in the Isle of Man. They were happy times, and the boys enjoyed the family atmosphere as much as I did. In all honesty, I hadn't been happy with Daniel being away at sea for long periods. The boys needed him home as much as I did. One of the hardest things I had to do was talk to him about the need for him to be at home with us. The sea and his job were important to him, and I knew that he had realised a dream he'd had since he was a young boy. I also knew that he might regret it if he left sea and came home to us for good. What can I say? I gave him a choice, hoping that it didn't sound like an ultimatum. As luck would have it, his company offered Voluntary Selective Severance with an attractive package, and I was delighted and relieved when he decided to accept. He was only home a short time when he found another job in engineering. We loved having him home but soon, all that was to change. His company asked him to go to work in Saudi Arabia. When he had worked there for almost a year, I told him I wasn't happy, and he returned home and found a job locally. His new job was known as a 'job for life' and I was very grateful for that. The boys were nine and eleven by then, and at last I was able to think about going back to work. I knew I would need to work part-time to fit in with looking after our family and our home. It had been so long since I had worked with the public, and I felt a little nervous. What would I do?

Returning to Work

Nervous and dressed in a lovely cornflower blue suit, I found myself having an interview for a part time job as salesperson in a Bridal Shop. I was delighted to be told I could start the following week. I would be selling beautiful wedding gowns and accessories in one of the most exclusive bridal houses in Northern Ireland. It was a wonderful way of returning to work after being at home for so long. What a change it was to cast off the jeans that had been my uniform at home and dress beautifully with my make-up and hair immaculate every time I went to work. I felt glamourous for the first time in ages, and it was great for my self-esteem. It felt good to be doing something for myself after so many years of being at home bringing up our children.

I expected the new job would be all hearts, flowers, love and romance. Yes, it was all of those things, but it could be stressful, at times. Prospective brides bring their anxiety with them to fittings and as such they need to be treated gently and constantly reassured that all will be well on the most important day of their lives. The price tags on the gowns amazed me and it was a surprise to hear the cost of some of the weddings. Listening to the future brides' wedding plans, the arrangements seemed to start at least a year in advance. They had the church and venue for the wedding reception to book and the bride's gown and bridesmaids' dresses to order as not everyone selected from the wide range we had in stock. Headdresses, veils, shoes and flowers had to be organised; after that, the list of things to do was endless. I smiled remembering how my own wedding had been arranged in less than two months; and yet, everyone said it was a wonderful day. However, it was lovely helping others to fulfil their dreams.

The work was interesting, and all was going well until the school holidays were almost upon us and I decided I needed to be at home for my boys. I explained the situation to my boss and told her I was leaving. I spent the summer with my boys and when they were about to return to school, my boss telephoned to ask me if I would come back to work. I was happy to, and this pattern continued for two years. After that I decided it was time to leave the bridal shop and have a break. I knew that it was unfair taking the two busiest months of the year off and it would then allow my boss to find someone who would be happy to work over the summer months.

It wasn't very long before I found that I missed

work. I also realised that the little bit of money of my own had given me independence. There was a large gift shop in the town, and I applied for a job there. I got the letter quite soon to tell me to start work. I was asked to vacuum the floor about two days after I started, and I wasn't too pleased about that! I was a salesperson and a good one and vacuuming wasn't part of my job description. (On an honest level, I felt like a bull in a china shop — with all of the expensive merchandise around, I was terrified of breaking something.) My attitude did not win me very many friends among the women who worked there, as apparently they all took turns at cleaning the floor. The fact that I was never asked to vacuum the floor again probably didn't please them either. I did, however, wash down shelves etc. as it helped me to familiarise myself with the stock. Everything we sold was of the highest quality — beautiful china, crystal glasses, silver cutlery, mirrors, pictures, ornaments and many household items. I worked hard and was always pleasant, but the frosty atmosphere was not one that I had ever encountered before — certainly not in the work place. I thought of leaving, but I also had a stubborn streak that made me persevere and eventually the women became friendlier towards me. I left at summer holiday time, and my boss always took me back in September, so I must have been doing my work to his satisfaction.

The experience in the gift shop was invaluable. I learned a lot about human nature and my own character, but I also learnt a lot about the finer things in life. Due to a good staff discount, I purchased some beautiful cutlery which I could never have afforded otherwise. After a couple of years there I decided to leave for good when the summer holidays came around for our boys. I didn't know it then, but something exciting was about to happen for us and I would need to be free to spend time on our next project.

The House with the Stunning Views

We had decided to move house earlier that year, but our house took a long time to sell. I remember thinking that Daniel's grandmother, who had been dead for about twelve years, didn't want us to move. We had found a beautiful house a couple of miles away, and we finally had a buyer for ours. The night before we left the house, the dishwasher came on in the middle of the night of its own accord. I imagined it was someone wanting to say goodbye. My brother-in-law owned the house next door to ours, which had also belonged to Daniel's grandmother, and when their family moved, the lights flashed off and on a few times during the night before they flitted to their new home.

Just before we left the house to move to the new one, we decided we would have a shopping trip to another town. It was to be a day out with our two sons, who were now in their teens, and we would do a bit of shopping and have lunch together. I got dressed up for the occasion and, at the last minute, put on the beautiful bracelet my husband had brought me from Dubai. It was a double rope of gold intertwined with white gold and it was the most beautiful piece of jewellery I had ever owned. I'd had it for three years, and I had seldom gone out without wearing it.

We had lunch as soon as we arrived in Lisburn, a town about twenty-five miles away, quite a drive from where we lived. After lunch, my husband and I went our separate ways, taking one son each with us. Alan, my eldest son, always accompanied me, and our youngest son, Gary, always went with his dad. Alan and I had finished our shopping and while we waited to meet up with the others, I was looking at the display in a jeweller's shop window. I spotted a ring priced at £5,000 and said to Alan, "Imagine a man loving a woman enough to buy that for her." Although it hadn't cost anything like that, I remembered Daniel had loved me enough to give me my bracelet. Smiling, I looked down at my wrist and my husband's lovely present was gone! Well, I was in such a state of despair. Daniel and our sons patiently traipsed around the shops with me, retracing every footstep, but to no avail. I had to admit I had lost it. Before we left the town, we placed an advert in the local paper saying there was a reward for whoever found it. We checked with the Police to see if it had been handed in, but it had not. We came home and I cried for three days about the loss of it. I couldn't accept that I would never see it again. After looking in the car, I searched the house. What if it had come off before we went shopping? We checked the auction of lost property that the police have every few months to no avail. My lovely bracelet was gone! I was glad I had worn it almost every day of the three years I'd had it — wouldn't it have been worse if I had only got to enjoy it a handful of times? At least, that is what I told myself to ease the pain of losing it. We were all OK, no one was ill, no one had died, it was a bracelet at the end of the day, and I comforted myself with these thoughts just like most people would have done. I don't know if I will ever find out what happened to it, but it is a mystery I would love to solve before I die.

While I was distraught about its loss someone told me about a fortune teller who was working in the Ghost Room of Ballygally Castle. To cheer myself up I decided to pay her a visit. Climbing the spiral staircase to the Ghost Room, I felt a bit nervous. As a young girl my mother had worked as a chambermaid in the castle and she told me the room was scary and the staff would only go in to clean it, in pairs.

I approached the door with trepidation, but a beautiful young woman asked me to enter and put me at ease almost immediately. She began to read my palm, and then suddenly she stopped and said, "I can find things for people, you know." I looked at her with what must have been a puzzled expression. Almost immediately I exclaimed, "My bracelet, I have lost my bracelet." As I talked, she picked up a pendulum and soon it was swinging to and fro in her hand. I didn't understand, but she was mentally asking questions as to where my bracelet might be. The pendulum was giving her 'yes' or 'no' answers, which she understood by the way it was swinging. Suddenly she said, "Your bracelet is not lost. It is in your house somewhere. I can come to your house and find it for you." I didn't know this woman, and, if I am honest, I was a little afraid of something I didn't really understand. I was okay about going to visit psychics, but I am now ashamed to say I didn't want to invite them to my house. Deep down I suppose I was a product of my Christian upbringing, after all. I thanked her but said it was okay; I would leave it and the bracelet might turn up.

A short time after we moved into our new house, we visited the couple who had bought our old house. I told them the story about my bracelet. They searched the house from top to bottom, but they did not find my bracelet. I did not expect them to find it as I felt we had taken everything with us when we moved, but it was kind of them to look. More than thirty-five years have passed and I have never found my bracelet, but I would dearly love to see it again.

One good thing came out of it all — Daniel and I became great friends with the couple who bought our old house. After they had been living there for a while, the lady, who had a direct way of speaking, asked, "Did you know this house was haunted before you sold it to us?" Well, I didn't know how to answer, so I said, "Why do you say that?" She said, "I am a clairvoyant and I sometimes smell fish in the house. I think a fisherman lived here at one time. I don't mind; in fact, if you had told me it was haunted, I might have given you more money for it." She was laughing, but I was relieved that she had not been scared by anything. I really wanted her to be as happy in her home as we were in our new house. One thing bothered me, though — when we moved to our new house, I woke up in a panic one time, feeling that a fluffy white cat was lying on my chest. I was having trouble breathing. Could I have dreamt it? I never did find out if the people who lived in the house before us had a white cat.

The Castle

Our new home had beautiful sea views, but it needed a lot of work to update it. We had only just moved in when the electricity went off. It happened several times, and we couldn't figure out the reason. I took it personally, and, in tears, I said to Daniel "I don't think this house likes us." He told me everything would be fine once he found out why it was happening. He came into the house one day looking victorious, a smile spread across his handsome features. "One of the outside lights is full of water, and that is probably why the electricity is going off," he said. I was relieved when he sorted it out. However, the house was plunged into darkness again that evening. I was upset as we had invited my mother, stepfather and two of my brothers for dinner during the Christmas holidays. I couldn't risk having the oven go off when I was cooking the turkey. Finally, we discovered it was the fault of a television set we had brought from our previous house. Once Daniel fixed the problem, peace reigned again. We had no time to decorate before Christmas, but we made the house look as nice as possible. I displayed the Christmas cards in the form of curtains around the window in the lounge, and once the tree was decorated and a nice log fire had been lit, the room looked as if we had been living there for ages. I smiled as I surveyed it, and the thought came to me that I was as good as my grandmother at being resourceful. I was pleased that I was a good home maker.

After Christmas, work on the house began. I sanded the walls until they were as smooth as silk and then we painted them. Daniel used a wood chisel to scrape the old dark varnish off the window frames and then he used a much lighter varnish on them. When we had been working constantly on the place for six months, I felt we had made a wonderful difference. However, in order to make our home as nice as we wanted it to be, we would need to spend a lot more money on it. There was only one way we would be able to afford the little extras and that was if I found a job. I told my husband I was going out to find work, and he laughed. I don't think he thought it would be that easy. However, I applied for a job as a tour guide in a castle that was situated in a nearby town, and I was pleased when I got a temporary place for three months. It was a well-paid job and just what I was looking for.

I began to work there, and the first thing I had to do was follow another tour guide around for three of the tours by way of training. Studying the history of the castle in my own time left me feeling confident enough to give tours quite quickly. It was a wonderful job, especially if you enjoy meeting people of all nationalities and from every walk of life. Like the other tour guides, I took different groups around the castle, from pre-school age children to primary, secondary, college and university students. One minute you could be giving a tour to a group of Woman's Institute and the next it might be a rowdy football or rugby team. We could be showing many people around, from individuals to family groups, celebrities to Government Ministers; although there wasn't anyone who was treated as being any more important than anyone else. People have asked me whether I found it boring going over the same thing day in and day out and that was never the case; I found my personality changing to accommodate each tour, and instinctively I knew what would interest each group. The work was exhausting, but I loved it.

There was also another side to working there. People got married in the little chapel, which held groups of about twenty-seven. Receptions and banquets were held in the keep of the castle and it was lovely to feel a part of those. Exhibitions were held there as well. Medieval Fairs were a favourite with the public and staff alike. The castle really came to life then with stalls of every kind as well as archery, mummers, jousting etc. It was easy to imagine how the castle would have been in Norman times. Children loved having their birthday parties in the dungeons, and the time I worked there was a brilliant time in the castle's history. It had been a military museum for quite some time, and suddenly, after a makeover, fun had returned to the castle once more. I am sure you are wondering if all of this happened in the course of the three months I worked there. The answer is — of course not! I talked so much that I was employed there for two years!

I remember a time when talking became a problem. I had been taking so many tours around the castle that I lost my voice. My doctor advised me to have two weeks off work to rest and gave me what was then known as a sick line. While I was off work, I realised I had booked an appointment to attend a floristry workshop in my hometown and the date for it fell within the time of my sick leave. My friend Nancy and I had been looking forward to it as we were to be shown how to decorate a Christmas tree and Mantelpiece, as well as making table centrepieces and other decorations. These were lessons we could use for the rest of our lives I reasoned, and I could be quiet and rest my voice, couldn't I? Yes, I would go, and nobody need ever know. How wrong I was! I should have known I would never get away with it.

The room was fragrant with the aroma of pine branches and flowers and bundles of fairy lights. Church candles and baubles, with not even a hint of gaudiness, were displayed on tables as we sipped our tea and coffee before starting. I was admiring all of this and thinking of my own much loved but inexpensive bits and pieces, including the decorations the children had made at school, when the photographer from the local newspaper came into the room to take a few photographs of the event. My heart skipped a beat, and my face must have turned white as a sheet. I looked at Nancy in panic, as if she might have the answer to my dilemma. Finding only a sympathetic smile on her face, I knew I would have to own up to my predicament. Taking my place in the line-up for the photograph, I said, "I am off work, on the sick!" Well, everyone laughed and as their laughter flowed around the room it certainly broke the ice. Next day, I telephoned my boss at the castle and explained what had happened. He saw the funny side of it, and said as long as I had rested my voice it was ok. Thank goodness he had been so understanding, for a moment I thought I might be facing the sack.

During my time at the castle, I made lots of new friends. The other tour guides were great raconteurs and we had so much fun. We socialised together and many a good story was told when we went to the local inn. Sometimes as we sipped our hot port, to warm us after a cold winter's day at work, the conversation would turn to whether we believed in or had encountered the castle ghost. It was said that a young soldier who had been stationed in the castle in the eighteenth century had been wrongly accused of having an affair with the wife of his Captain's brother. His punishment was execution and many people believe that he can be heard wailing his innocence to this day. Although I had often felt nervous when I was checking and locking up the keep in the dark nights of winter, I can honestly say I had never seen anything unusual. The draughts I felt, like someone blowing cold air on my face or neck — well, that was just the wind, wasn't it? The shrill sounds I heard — well, you get those in an old building, don't you?

Our house had a little bar in it, and we often invited our friends from work to it for a party. It was a great time in our lives — the boys were in their teens by then and they loved to play pool and generally enjoy the fun we had together. They enjoyed our company so much that when they found girlfriends, they all preferred to stay at home with us in the evenings instead of going out as young people do. The house was looking well with all the hard work and the money we spent on it, and we were proud to show it off to our friends. It had been turned into a beautiful home and we basked in the compliments of all the people who visited. All good things come to an end, so they say, and I'm afraid to say the same was about to happen for us.

I had begun working at the castle on a three-month contract, which kept being extended until I was there for two years. Unfortunately, that was to be the end of my time there, as the maximum time for a temporary contract was two years. I cried the day I left. It was the best job I had ever had. As I took off my lovely green uniform for the last time, there was a sense of losing a part of myself. I would no longer be part of a knowledgeable team who not only taught people the history of the castle and the town but also gave advice to tourists on how to make the most of their time in beautiful Northern Ireland. My friends from the castle and I had a little party in the old inn where we had spent happy times. I promised to keep in touch, but I knew that I would no longer be one of them. A wonderful part of my working life had ended. It was the perfect job — imagine talking all day and being paid for it! I had been so used to being with people, I knew I wouldn't be happy at home alone while Daniel was at work and the boys were at College. What on earth would I do next?

Country House Accommodation

The answer came to me much quicker than expected. We had a wonderful house with amazing sea views on one side and rural views on the other. We also had two spare bedrooms and a bathroom on the top floor. What if we were to share our home with others? If we were to take in paying guests for bed and breakfast I knew they would love it, but what about me? Wouldn't I have to cook breakfast for them? I had never cooked in the professional sense for anyone before and my culinary skills were definitely limited to family meals. During the course of my life, we had travelled to many places; we had dined out a lot and I knew the standard that would be expected by paying guests. Would a continental breakfast of cereal, toast, croissants, ham, cheese, fruit and jams suffice? No, this was Northern Ireland — people would expect a cooked breakfast, bacon, egg, sausage, mushrooms, tomatoes, soda bread and potato bread, at the very least. I could manage that; after all, I had cooked the famous Ulster Fry for the family at least once a fortnight. Suddenly I realised I could make a bed and breakfast business work. I was still young — in my forties — and I wasn't afraid of hard work.

Just to be on the safe side, I took a small business course. I was nervous when I walked into the room and saw that quite a few of the men there had brought their computers with them. I had a pen and a notebook! During the course, I discovered that I would need to inform the Tourist Board of my intentions. After paying a fee, they took me under their wing, and the rest was easy. I had a visit from the Fire Service to check the safety of the property, which was fine. Public Health also paid a visit; they checked my fridge and freezer temperatures and gave me a food hygiene quiz. Again, all was fine and since I was only doing things in a small way, I was allowed to have my certificate to say the property was suitable for Bed and Breakfast.

I ran the Bed and Breakfast for eight years, and, during that time, we had many guests, beginning with just a few in the first year and increasing to quite a lot in the latter years. Every year we wondered who would come to stay with us — it was really exciting. I loved it — new people every year with some of them returning again and again, like old friends.

Our first guests were poets who were going to a creative writing weekend in the area. Unwittingly, I had given one young man inspiration for a poem. I had only one rule and that was that there was no smoking allowed in the house. I explained this and showed the young man where he could smoke. One evening I was invited to the poet's house for the readings, which I was enjoying immensely until my guest stood up and began his poem. He coughed a little nervously and then he said, "The smoker goes to his little designated area …." I had no doubt that the poem was directed at me, but I smiled sweetly through it. We obviously had very different views about smoking in the house.

The poets and writers we had staying with us were lovely, and, if I am honest, I felt a little envious of them. It seemed as if they did not have a care in the world — or, if they did, they turned it into a story and made the most of it. When they set off after breakfast, I wished I was going too. Yet, it was to be many years before I would go to a writer's workshop or have my short stories published. It was a workshop that gave me the courage to sit down and write the story of my life in, *Beyond the Sallagh Braes*.

The poets brought something different to my world. An American lady came to stay for a fortnight, and, before she went to the poet's house, she asked me if she looked grungy enough. She was wearing a dull sweater under black dungarees. I asked what she meant and she said, "I will be judged on what I am wearing, and I need to appear serious."

It was something I would never have given any thought to. A well-known Irish writer in his later years came to stay, and he brought a beautiful young girl of eighteen with him. I assumed she was his daughter, but he introduced her as his muse. My face must have looked a picture because I hadn't a clue what he was talking about. I had to ask if they needed one room or two, but I can't tell you what they chose because a good landlady would never reveal something like that.

We were fortunate that we only seemed to get nice guests, as I am sure that may not always be the case for others. Tourists came from all over the world. There was the little family from Iran who arrived at the door after 11.00 pm one dark night. (As a rule I didn't take late arrivals). We were in bed when the doorbell rang and I sent my husband to answer the door, telling him to say no if it was someone wanting accommodation. He came back to the bedroom and told me he thought we should take these guests. I got up grudgingly and went to the door, but I relented when I saw them on the doorstep. I didn't have the heart to turn them away.

Another time, a young German couple were quite furtive when they were checking in. I wondered about them until I went to make up their room next day and saw they had a camping stove and frying pan set up on the dressing table. They wanted to stay an extra night, but I felt they were a fire risk, so I had to say no.

Everyone who stayed had a story to tell, and I was privileged to hear some of them. An older man visited from New Zealand. Originally, he had lived in Belfast, but he had been evacuated to an area near us as a child during the Second World War. This was the case with a lot of city children, who were sent to the country for safety. I have often wondered how those poor children must have felt leaving their parents to go and live with complete strangers. The farmer this man stayed with had treated him like a slave and worked him from dawn until dusk. He told me there was no love in the house even though he was separated from his brothers and sisters, who had been sent elsewhere. Most of them, he never saw again. Returning to Belfast after the war, he then immigrated to New Zealand, where he had done well for himself. All of those years had passed, and at the turn of the century, he had come to Ireland for a holiday and decided to see if the farmer was still alive and if he remembered him. He wanted to thank him for taking him into his home in the time of war. I never heard if the two men met up, as the man left next day intending to see the farmer and continue on his travels. His story taught me a lesson in forgiveness and gratitude.

A couple in their sixties stayed one night and

asked if they could extend their stay for another night. The lady told me her husband had traced his birth mother, and she had agreed to meet him. They left that evening to meet the woman and some of her family for dinner in a local hotel. I was surprised when I got a call to ask if they could come back to stay for another night. The man's mother had changed her mind, and they were heartbroken and couldn't face travelling the long distance home. It was just as well they stayed that night —the man's mother changed her mind again and agreed to meet them next morning. They were happy when they were leaving and by then I felt we had been through so much together. I threw my arms around them and hugged them. It was lovely to have a story with a happy ending.

There were lots of guests who were fun as well, like the young Australian man who left early in the morning. He was travelling to a Druid's Altar where he had planned to lie on top of it like a sacrifice waiting for sunrise. Since it had rained a lot in Northern Ireland in the previous few days, I was hoping he wouldn't have too long to wait! We had lots of contractors who were working locally staying also. Sometimes I had to provide dinner for them as well as bed and breakfast and a packed lunch. We had four young men from Scotland staying for a few weeks, and I noticed that they were not eating the vegetables I was giving them. I enquired what was wrong with them and they told me there was nothing wrong. They explained, "if it disnae come oot o a tin, we havnae had it." I asked what they meant, and they said their mothers had not given them real vegetables, like broccoli, carrots and turnip — they just got tinned peas, beans etc. The menu had to be revised, which saved me a lot of work on the preparation of dinner.

A French man booked in for a couple of nights. He was in his sixties, perhaps — well dressed, suave and sophisticated. At breakfast time he smiled and said, "*Vous est très jolie madame.*" Later, repeating what he said, I told my mother-in-law that my guest thought I was a very happy woman. She said that was not what he meant, at all, — he was saying, "You are a very pretty woman." She finished our conversation by saying, "I would watch him if I were you." Oops! Perhaps I should have paid more attention to those French lessons at school.

I remember the afternoon some Italians arrived with us. Two old men, who had never been out of their village in Italy before, sat at my dining room table looking bewildered. They didn't speak one word of English and neither did the three young men who accompanied them. At least the younger men were smiling and looked as if they might become acclimatised to their new surroundings. One of the younger men did not adapt well to our wet May weather after leaving the sunshine of Italy. He greeted me every morning with the words "Nostalgia Italia, no sole" which I took to mean, "Homesick for Italy, no sunshine." The Italians didn't speak English and I didn't speak their language, so it was with the help of phrase books that we had to converse. You cannot have people staying in your home for any length of time and not make an effort to talk to them. Near the end of their stay, every time I picked up the phrase book, they all began laughing and chorused, "Speak, speak madam." Once a week we took them to an Italian Restaurant. The man who made the pizzas there was from Sicily, so it gave the guests a chance to have real Italian food and speak to someone in their own language. As a family, we joined them at the dining table sometimes, and, in my limited way, I tried to provide them with Italian food. I quickly discovered they started dinner with salad and bread. Then, I alternated a few pasta dishes with delicious sauces and meat, lamb or chicken. Most evenings they had a bottle of wine, but they insisted I have the first glass. I remember thinking they had better not stay too long or I would be in danger of becoming an alcoholic! My husband looked longingly at their meals and said, "I want to be an Italian!"

One evening, an old friend joined us for dinner.

He had been to Italy during World War II. He was so happy to be invited and he brought along some of his paperwork from that time to show them. Being excited, he talked quickly in the little bit of Italian he remembered. The men were very kind to him and for that I shall always be grateful. I attended his funeral a short time later, and I was surprised when the minister said how delighted the old man had been to have spent the evening with us. I realised that it is sometimes the little things we do that mean so much to others. We enjoyed having the Italians to stay — somehow, we managed to communicate, but it was a relief when they went home and I could go back to speaking English again.

Then there was the Irishman who was a digger driver. When I gave him his dinner at night, he carefully moved it around the plate with his fork until it was piled up in the middle. Satisfied with this rearrangement, he would say "Will I just work away, Morna?" I smiled knowing it was the same way he had been approaching the loads of soil on the building site all day. During the time he stayed with us, he and one of his co-workers came home one night to be told the electricity was off. My husband had lit a big roaring fire and the room was glowing with the light from oil lamps and candles. It reminded me of my childhood. Since I had lived through a time when electricity had not existed in our home, I didn't find it too much of a problem to be without it. I cooked a pot of Irish stew on the little gas cooker, and we sat around the fire and ate bowls of it accompanied by soda bread and glasses of milk. With a couple of whiskies to follow we all told great stories and the conversation flowed until bedtime. Again, this reminded me of those times in my childhood. As for the men, they agreed it was the best night they had had in a long time.

If all of this sounds exciting and you would love to do as I did and start offering Bed and Breakfast to tourists and contractors, please be aware that the work is extremely hard — do not let anyone tell you otherwise. I remember one morning cooking breakfast for five contractors and knowing I had to make packed lunches for them to take to work, when the telephone on the kitchen table started ringing. It was my youngest son Gary, asking if his jeans were through the wash yet. Surprised to hear his voice, I asked where he was ringing from, and he said he was in his bedroom. I told him he would have to come and look as I was too busy and some of the laundered clothes in the utility room consisted of washing I had been doing for the men also. Thankfully his jeans were ready, but, smiling cheekily, he told me not to forget he was a regular customer, and, as such, he should have priority!

The Unexpected Guest

When we had been keeping guests for a couple of years, a strange thing happened to me one morning. We had tourists staying mostly but also contractors who were working in the area. I was up early in the mornings, and I was tired sometimes. One morning after everyone, including my husband, had gone out to work, I decided I would go back to bed to catch up on some sleep. I locked the inner doors between our part of the house and the area we were using for guest accommodation. Gratefully sinking into the bed, which was warm and cosy, I soon found myself in that lovely state between waking and sleeping when it happened!

Someone — a male presence — came into the room. He moved around to the back of the bed and I could feel pressure on the bed as he sat down. I sensed him watching me, but I couldn't wake up properly. When I managed to wake up, there was nobody there. I checked to make sure the house had been locked the way I had left it before sleeping. Everything was just as it had been. Who was the man who sat on my bed watching me sleep? He had to be a Spirit. Was he my Guardian Angel? Was he the spirit of one of my ancestors, or a spirit belonging to the house? In the beginning I didn't mention it to anybody, thinking it was a one off — or, perhaps, my overactive imagination playing tricks on me.

If only that had been true! It started happening often, and I was afraid. I decided I would turn to the clairvoyant lady who had bought our previous house. She listened intently with a little smile on her face. "When you are awake and going about your work during the day, just ask aloud who it is and what do they want." "Oh no," I said. "I couldn't do that. What if someone answered?" I almost whispered. She laughed. "There is nothing to be afraid of. Write a little note asking those questions and leave it on your pillow before you go to sleep." I looked at her as if she had lost the plot, shocked at her suggestion. I said, "If I woke to find spidery writing on the bottom of my note, I would have a heart attack." Well, she laughed so heartily I had to join in.

Next time I visited, she asked me if it was still happening, and I pretended it hadn't happened again. Whoever was sitting on my bed wasn't doing me any harm — he was only looking at me. But I wasn't planning to have a conversation with him. That would have been too much.

I found the answer to my question about who he

was in the strangest way. My husband and I went to Hawaii for a holiday, and I paid a visit to a Clairvoyant in a market there. My visit to her was spontaneous and I was surprised when she was able to see me without an appointment. I was so busy looking at her strange eyes, deciding the irises held no colour that I didn't quite hear what she was saying. I had to ask her to repeat what she had just said. She told me I had brought a well-dressed man with me in Spirit. She said he was an educated man, and he had been trying to get through to his daughter and family but without success. "You have no need to fear him, he means you no harm," she told me. Apparently, he looked on me as a daughter and was protective towards me. I was relieved to hear all this, and, at the time, I wondered if the man was my husband's father, who had passed away shortly after we were married. After that visit to the Clairvoyant, I stopped worrying, and the times I sensed him became fewer.

Life had been very busy over the eight years I was doing Bed and Breakfast, and the time had gone so quickly that my boys were in their twenties before I knew it. My husband had the chance of taking early retirement from work when he was fifty. I had grown tired of all the work I was doing, although we had wonderful holidays during that time. We had been to Tenerife several times, and Malta, Corfu,

Rhodes, The Gambia, Cuba and Hawaii. However, we knew it was time for a change, and, after discussing it at length, we decided we would move to Tenerife. We flew there and had a fortnight's holiday, during our time there we went house-hunting, but we decided we would maybe get more property for our money in mainland Spain. Our eldest son, Alan, had already moved into a place of his own, so we decided we would buy a house with our youngest son, Gary, get him settled, and then we would move to Spain to start our new life.

We put our house up for sale, and, although it took some time to sell, we knew we would soon be on our way to fulfilling our dreams. With the help of our son, we viewed many properties in the area and found the perfect house where he could make a home and we could stay for holidays each time we returned from Spain. Together we purchased the lovely four-bedroomed house that we knew our son would be happy living in. We would be content thinking of him there while we went off to live in Spain.

Moving to Spain

We bought a house on the outskirts of an old Spanish village, after much house hunting, and we were glad to get moved into it. Our life in the sun was all we had hoped for, even if we'd had a few challenges along the way with the language and living with a new culture. Family and friends visited, and we made new friends of many nationalities. We were very sociable — we could afford to dine out three or four times each week as the food was reasonably priced. We also met friends for drinks in the village. The sun shone, the skies were blue almost every day and life was good.

I say the sun shone almost every day, but now and again we would get a two-day period when it rained, and occasionally there was thunder and lightning. It was during such a thunderstorm that we found ourselves driving to the Notary's office to make our Last Will and Testament. After buying the property, we had been advised to do this. Upon entering the Notary's office, our solicitor met us and asked us if we had remembered to bring our passports. Daniel had his with him as drivers are required by law to carry their passport or at least a copy of it. Mine was back at the house ten minutes' drive away. Our solicitor told us to go and pick it up and she would stall the Notary until we got back. She gave me copies of our wills in English to read and be prepared to sign when we returned saying it would save time. So, there we were, Daniel driving at quite a speed in the heavy rain and the thunder and lightning with me reading his Last Will and Testament to him. It wasn't funny at the time, but after we had conducted our business we found it hilarious.

This incident also made me think of our mortality, something I hadn't done when we made out our wills in the U.K. Perhaps it was being in a different country and living apart from our sons that had me thinking this way. That night, sitting outside one of little bars in the village after having a couple of glasses of wine, I asked one of our friends if he had given any thought as to what he intended to do if something happened to him or his partner while living in Spain. He was an East Ender with a great sense of humour, and as I had expected, he didn't take my question too seriously. No sooner had I spoken than the bin lorry came into view, passing through the village, emptying the bins at eleven o'clock as it did every night. Our friend said, "When I die here, the bin men are my friends and they can take me away in their lorry to the Crem., darling." I realised he meant the Crematorium and I thought, what a funeral that would be! I laughed with him, but it didn't stop me thinking about what would happen if I died in a strange country. That wasn't all; I didn't know what would happen to my Soul. Would I go to Heaven or Hell? I hoped it would be the former but how could I be sure?

We had arrived in Spain with two suitcases and neither of them contained a Bible. Just the previous day, I had mentioned this to my husband. With Easter due the following week, I wasn't quite sure of the order in which everything had happened leading up to the Crucifixion of Jesus Christ. We were on our way to an Internet Café in another town, and, as soon as we went inside, I began looking at the second hand books they had on sale. They had about thirty books on a mixture of topics as you would expect. I was really surprised when amongst them I found a Gideon's Bible. Of course, I added it to the collection I had selected, paid for them and took them home. Someone had answered my prayers without me even asking!

With Spain being a Catholic country, Easter is a very important date on their calendar. It is a time of fasting and sacrifice during Lent and then feasting to celebrate the fact that although Christ was crucified and died on the cross for our sins He arose from the dead three days later. People go to church for thanks giving. Families get together for most of the Easter holiday, picnicking, barbequing and generally having a good time. At these times, we missed our family very much. Friends become the family we have left behind, we told ourselves, but it wasn't quite true. They ease the loneliness, but nobody knows you like your own family. Of course, we had visits from friends and family, but it was not the same as having them in our lives full-time.

Before leaving Northern Ireland, looking after a family as well as guests had been a lot of work and I didn't give much thought to how I was feeling about the big questions. In Spain, while I was lying on a sunbed, or drifting on a lilo on top of the pool in the afternoon sun, I had time to think about the meaning of life and why we are on the Earth. I suppose you could say it gave me time to just be myself without outside distractions. I don't know that I formed any conclusions, but it was nice to wonder about such things. Why did I have to get to fifty years old before I met the man who told me I was a Healer? Now I was going to have to ask myself those big questions again and I didn't know where to start.

I had been living in Spain with my husband for three years when I met Kenny, the man who told me I was a healer. In the eight weeks that followed, a lot happened. Our house had been for sale for some time, and it had just been sold and soon we would return to Northern Ireland. I wasn't just packing to leave a way of life; I was leaving as a different person. I needed to visit the Healer as often as I could to gain some idea of what healing involved before leaving this knowledgeable man behind. Why were we going back home when we loved living in Spain? Like a lot of the people who move to a new country, we missed our family. To coin a well-known phrase "Blood is thicker than water." Oh, the ties that bind. We needed to return to the family we loved. Our adventure had come to an end.

Returning to Northern Ireland

My husband and I returned to N. Ireland and moved into the house we part-owned with our son. After Christmas, the house hunt began for a place of our own. We found a beautiful bungalow, not too far from where our son lived; we bought it and moved into it. I had been busy for a while settling in but thoughts of being a healer were always on my mind. My husband and sons were supportive, but, like me, it was something that they didn't know a lot about. My youngest son got me information from the internet, and I read every word, soaking it up like a sponge.

As far as I could see, there were different types of healing. Divine Healing was the type you got in church, but did that mean I had to be Holy all the time? I couldn't bear to have people judging me. As far as I could tell, Divine Healing was the Laying on of Hands, and a part of me wondered if I was good enough. I had no doubt there was an amazing amount of energy coming through my hands, but what about my connection with God? I went to church occasionally, but I didn't read the Bible often and I certainly didn't know it well.

I prayed at night and each morning, asking God to protect me and keep me safe. I asked Him to make me a good Healer. Family were included in my prayers and also those who were in need of healing. I started reading a little bit from the Bible every day. A feeling of warmth came over me, and I now realise I was living in God's grace. A lot of what was happening around me seemed to wash over me, whereas before I would have worried about it. I knew there was no point in worrying — everything happens for a reason, and hopefully we learn from the lessons that are put before us. I also learned that everything happened in God's timing, not mine. I felt that I was calmer than before.

At this point, I decided to meditate. In the beginning, I found it quite hard to still my mind. My monkey brain would chatter with all the things I had to do etc. I thought of things from the past and things yet to happen in the future, but I found it hard to just sit there, focus on my breathing and be in that moment in time. I played gentle music, thinking that it would help if I just lay and listened to it. I fell asleep! Eventually, I found my way into meditation completely by accident. One night I decided to close my eyes and pray, repeating prayers I had learned as a child. I was surprised at how well this method worked. Soon, I was in a quiet space, and it was as if I was wrapped in a warm pink blanket of Love. Continuing this way at night for some time, the most unusual thing happened...

My meditation went as follows. Before me was a white staircase. It was wide and swept up to the left. As I looked at it, someone was descending, someone in long flowing robes. I stared in amazement as Jesus descended. He looked just as I was used to seeing him in pictures. He held out His hands to me, and I was overcome with emotion. I knew that in the meditation, I was on my knees.

The same thing happened every day for a week. Each time it happened, He gave me a gift. I dropped my head and humbly accepted what I was given. I cannot say what He gave me, and I understand totally if you find all of this hard to believe. If someone else had told me this story, I would have found it hard to believe also. In all my time going to church, I don't ever remember being told that something like this could happen. The whole thing took me completely unawares, and I was in awe of what had happened to me.

I wanted to be alone with all that was happening. I wanted to be alone with my thoughts. Although I wasn't a Roman Catholic, I wondered if I should go into a Convent. I thought long and hard about it, and I decided that in order to grow, I needed to be out in the world. I needed to face up to life's everyday challenges, problems and solutions. I knew that my healing energy was meant to be among the people. I also knew that I was no more important than anyone else; we are all here for a reason. I was reminded of a Shakespearian quote I had heard, "All the world is a stage and the people merely players." It was the first time I had given any thought to it and now it made sense. We all have a part to play while we are here. We are like threads in a tapestry.

One thing I was certain of was that I needed a quiet space where I could be alone at times. Daniel had started apologising when he walked into a room and realised I was saying my prayers or meditating, and I didn't want him to feel uncomfortable in our home. Since the two of us lived in a three-bedroomed bungalow, I decided I could have a room for myself.

Right from the beginning, it became known as my quiet room. We decorated the room by painting it in pale cream. The carpet and curtains were the same colour. By the time we were finished, it had already taken on a feeling of peace. I hung beautiful golden tasselled tie backs on the curtains, giving them an air of opulence. A mahogany Victorian sideboard, chaise longue and matching chair completed the furnishings. When it was accessorised with pictures, gold lamps and candles, I knew it was somewhere very special — a place I could look forward to spending a lot of time in. With the addition of a healing couch and a spare chair, I knew it was somewhere I could invite others to when they were in need of healing. I went on to instinctively add crystals, incense and music, and the energy in the room felt wonderful. I felt we had truly created the perfect space to invite the Angels in to assist with the healing process and to guide me during my meditations.

I am sure you are wondering if all of this was really necessary — or, can healing be done anywhere? The answer is yes, healing can be done anywhere, and most people with the gift of healing are prepared to work anywhere. Some healers prefer to work in a room with only a healing couch and a couple of chairs. Visiting Coleraine, a town on the Antrim coast, I saw healers from a local church working in the open air. They had a row of chairs placed near the Town Hall and anyone who wished to have healing was invited to take a seat. The healers looked very serene while they worked and there was a feeling of peace around the whole area. At the time, I remember thinking it was a great example of the church serving the people, and I wished that all churches would do the same — their love and compassion could stretch out to communities all over the world. What if this was like dropping a pebble in water and the ripples spread out to infinity?

I have received healing myself in the Presbyterian Church and the Spiritualist Church, and a wonderful peace and calmness came over me while the healing was being administered. I have also received it at Mind Body Spirit Fairs, usually in a quiet corner away from everything else that was taking place. I know that healers also work in hospitals in cooperation with the wonderful doctors and nurses already doing everything they can for their patients. It is my greatest wish that healers may continue to do more of this: NHS staff has never needed assistance more than today.

I knew that the time might come when I might be required to work in this way, but in the beginning, I felt I would need to build up my confidence by working alone in my quiet space. I would use it for prayer and meditation and be guided by whatever was to follow.

I bought so many books! I felt drawn to buy some of them — in fact, I could not leave the bookshop without them. Others I bought because the subjects were of interest to me. I bought books about healing, other religions, self-help, mediumship, crystals and Angel card reading. Looking back, I think I was trying to put myself in a box. Which category did I fit into? The nearest I came to someone who sounded like me was a Christian Spiritualist. I believed whole-heartedly in God as the Father, Son and Holy Spirit, but I also believed strongly in other aspects of the Spiritualist Church — aspects that the Christian churches I had visited had not touched upon. For example, I believe that it is possible for departed spirits to communicate with us here on the Earth. I also feel that there are spirits who are dedicated to the welfare and service of mankind.

I went through a very special transformation. I began to see the beauty on our Earth. Landscapes became stunning. And, in my mind, I thanked God for the wonderful world we take for granted every day. Thinking of the variety of scenery and the different climates that it took to maintain everything on our planet amazed me. Nature, in all of its glory, was fascinating; I gave thanks for the flora and fauna, and I began examining things as if I was seeing them for the first time. I gave a great deal of thought to man and the inventions and advancements he has made, especially in the last hundred years. Did all of this come at a cost to our fragile Earth? I found that I was a little bored with ordinary small talk. Why couldn't people talk about issues that mattered? I didn't dare say any of this, of course. I began feeling a bit disconnected from everyone — a bit lonely.

My dreams became more vivid. I remembered them when I woke, trying to give meaning to them.

In fact, I started looking for the meaning in everything: so many things seemed like coincidences. I started seeing the rights and wrongs before me in a way that was non-judgmental. I observed in order to learn. Did I make mistakes? Of course I did. I had started looking at everything from a spiritual point of view, but, at the end of the day, I am in a human body just as everyone else is. We all have the ability to look at things from a spiritual point of view; I had a sense of all of us being on the same journey, learning the lessons on Earth with a view to being reunited with our Creator one day. I felt more sympathetic and understanding when I saw the suffering and problems people has to deal with. I suppose compassion had opened my heart. It was as if I became fully awake to all that had always been around me. I have asked myself over the years whether I am glad that I found out I was on my Spiritual Journey at that time. My answer has to be yes because of the joy in my heart.

I talked to a couple of my friends who were Christians. I didn't tell them of my meditation about Christ and it was just as well. I told them of my visit to the healer in Spain and how I felt God had called me to be a healer. They told me the Devil can also heal! A Born Again Christian asked me, "Why would God choose you?" I was hurt by her words and instead of thinking why would He not choose me, I thought — what if she was right? I had been given the wonderful proof of Jesus's existence in meditation and yet I had allowed the comment to undermine that. There are times when we all say things without thinking first and she has since told me that she did not mean to hurt me; she was just curious to know why I had been chosen.

I talked to another friend who was a Church Elder, and he suggested I speak to the minister. That didn't go so well either — I told him of my meditation experience and I knew by the way he looked at me that the same hadn't happened to him. He told me to be calm and that God could heal without me. He told me to be patient and wait. That was the last thing I wanted to hear, as I was keen to start using this wonderful gift. He offered to take me to see a healing service at St. Anne's Cathedral in Belfast one day, but it was short notice and I had promised to take an elderly gentleman out for lunch. I knew he was looking forward to it, and I could not disappoint him. I thanked the very kind minister for his offer and his help and that was the last I saw of him.

Although the Healer in Spain had given me some training in Spiritual Healing, I knew I hadn't the confidence to offer it to others just yet. A part of me felt humble as I knew I was an instrument that God's healing could come through but on my own I was not capable of healing others. I was going to have to find someone I could talk to about healing, someone who could make me feel I could introduce myself as a healer and be confident enough to work with the people who required my help. What was I supposed to do?

Reiki

I was reading the local newspaper when the answer came to me. There was the story of a young woman who had been injured as result of an accident. She had recovered from her injuries after having something called Reiki Healing. She had been so impressed that she had trained as a Reiki Master in order to facilitate healing for others. I decided I needed to find out more about this form of healing, so I telephoned her. She explained that Reiki is a traditional form of natural healing which goes back at least two and a half thousand years. It was rediscovered in the nineteenth century by a Japanese Monk called Dr Mikao Usui. The word Reiki means Universal Life Force Energy. This energy is in every living thing, and when it becomes depleted, problems with our health can occur. Once trained in this system of healing, it is possible to help balance the energy not only in our own body but in the bodies of others — as well as animals, plants and everything that has the life force within it. Reiki always works for the highest and greatest good and receiving it can lead to the well-being of the mind, body and spirit. This wonderful healing energy is channelled through the hands, and it can help to alleviate pain and deal with symptoms quickly. It supports and accelerates the body's natural ability to heal itself. As she talked, I listened, but I had already made up my mind that I would like to pursue the subject of Reiki further. It sounded as if it was exactly what I had been seeking.

She said that she would be teaching the First Degree in Reiki and I decided I would go along. Over the course of the weekend, I gained confidence by seeing the benefits of Reiki and by using it — not only on myself, but on others. The Second Degree course followed shortly after, and I went along for it as well. I met others with the same aims as myself, and I learned how to work with the people who would come to me for Reiki.

There was one difference between Reiki and Spiritual Healing that bothered me in the beginning. Spiritual Healing is free of charge, although donations may be gratefully accepted. However, there is usually an exchange of energy for a Reiki treatment. This does not have to be money — it can be an exchange of Complimentary Therapies, for example, or something agreed by the therapist and client. I found this hard to accept in the beginning. Let me tell you about a case study that changed my mind.

A man came to see me because of his back problems. I told him if he found the treatments helpful, I would give him the first six free of charge, but after that if he wished to have more, I would accept payment. He had six treatments free and then another six, but he didn't mention money and I didn't like to ask for payment. At that point, I said that in future I would accept payment. He made appointments for the following two weeks and didn't come; he didn't even get in touch to cancel. I realised I had handled the situation unprofessionally by not having a clear contract with him. Despite the fact his back had improved immensely, as well as his mental health, I felt he hadn't treated me respectfully. Even worse was the fact he seemed to have no respect for the wonderful energy that had eased his suffering. The money wasn't so important to me; it was the feeling that I had been used; it was the total disregard for the Reiki healing energy that hurt. I met him at a social occasion a few months later and he said Reiki had helped him and he would like to come back and see me. I explained that he could telephone for an appointment and I never heard from him again.

I discussed my reluctance to ask for payment with another Reiki Practitioner, and she explained it like this, "You have paid quite a lot for your training. You are giving the person the benefit of that experience. You are giving your time. That is no different to a hairdresser, a beautician, a doctor, a dentist, a member of the medical profession, or anyone else who is employed in providing a service to others." She also explained that it is not good for the person you are treating to feel as if they are in your debt. Instead of feeling bad about accepting money, she suggested I donate some of the payment to charity. After that I decided I would be clear about what was expected from the sessions with my clients. I also knew that there would be times when I would continue to work with people and not expect payment of any kind. I have worked with others in a healing centre treating people with Reiki for which I wouldn't have charged. I have never charged for short treatments or Distance Healing which is when the client cannot be present for one reason or another.

Once I had sorted out my feelings about payment it felt as if everything else just fell into place. When someone made an appointment, I explained what would happen when they arrived. I filled in a form with their details and reason for coming to see me. Other information was also taken — their medication, water intake, weekly alcohol consumption etc. After that I stated clearly that their first step should always be a visit to their doctor as Reiki is a complimentary therapy. When all of this had been conducted, they gave their consent for their treatment to begin. People came with a number of health complaints — back problems, infertility, anxiety, depression etc. They all seemed to benefit in some way from Reiki and left feeling much better than when they had arrived. I knew that the healing came from a higher source, but it gave me a good feeling to know that I had helped to facilitate that healing energy to others.

Angel Awareness Classes

While I was meeting up with the other members of my Reiki group, I learned of an Angel Awareness Group. I had no idea what to expect when I attended the first meeting, but I was pleasantly surprised to find I knew most of the people there from the Reiki Group. It was a small group of less than a dozen people sitting in a circle of chairs. The couple taking the group were brother and sister, and they were both lovely. Their friendliness and kindness put everyone at ease. It was while I was attending these evenings that I found out there was a name for people like me — I am a Light Worker. In other words, I feel that I am on the Earth to spread God's Love and Light, Peace and Healing in whatever way I can.

I learned a lot by attending the group about once a month for three years. During those evenings, I was reminded that everyone on the Earth has a Guardian Angel who cares for their Soul from before birth until after death, seeing them safely back to the Divine Source. During their time on Earth, other Angels may come to their assistance when required, but their Guardian Angel never leaves their side. God has given us free will, and we must ask the Angels for help before they can intervene in our lives. I smiled when I realised that there is a hierarchy of Angels, and it reminded me of the time when I thought of God as an old man sitting on His throne and all the Angels rushing around doing his bidding. The saying "As above, so below" refers to whatever happens in Heaven is reflected on Earth. Does that mean that although there is a hierarchy of Angels they are all equal in the sight of God, as we are?

The first Sphere and closest to God:

Seraphim, Cherubim and Thrones

The Second Sphere rule over the Earth:

Dominions, Virtues and Powers

The Third Sphere are guides, messengers and protectors:

They are Principalities, Archangels and Angels.
In Meditation, over a period of time, we were able to sense our Angels with us. Angels have different energies and once used to these, it is possible to know which ones are near us. Archangel Michael brings a wonderful warm energy to surround us.

I would sometimes feel feathers tickling my face, and I knew it was an indication that the Angels were near. For some people the energy feels lighter around them. Angels of Light always bring a sense of wellbeing to us. In the beginning, in meditation, Angels usually show themselves as we expect them to be. They appear to have a human form that is usually quite beautiful. They seem either male or female, but they are neither. They appear this way in order not to frighten us, and once we are used to working with them, they may change in appearance. Sometimes they are seen as orbs of Light. I have seen them as little twinkling stars; it is like looking out into the universe. I have also seen beautiful symbols that I know from looking at Angel books are associated with them. They may make their presence known as different colours of light. These are just a few of the ways they show themselves to us and I am sure there are many more.

At our Angel Awareness classes we learned how to send healing as a group. We called in the Angels and asked for their healing which is very powerful. We sent it on to people and also situations and countries where it was needed most. It gave me a great feeling of relief to know that I was doing something to help instead of just worrying, which doesn't solve anything.

We were told to look out for signs from the Angels. Some people get feathers in the most unexpected places, many keep finding small coins. For others it can be Angel numbers. These are numbers which are usually repeated, an example is 11.11

on a digital clock being noticed often. There are books about Angel Numbers, and it is also possible to Google and ask for the meaning of them. When I asked the Angels for a sign that they were near me I kept finding little foil hearts everywhere. It was such a comforting feeling to know that we are never alone; the Angels are always with us.

The Angels can also communicate with us through Angel Cards which can be purchased easily. I loved it when I got my first pack and looked at the beautiful pictures. A little book of messages accompanied them, and the messages were always positive. The more we read the cards for each other in the group, the better we became at understanding their meanings. Another time, I went to an Angel Card Reading course in the South of Ireland. It was being given by a well-known Angel Card Reader and it was combined with a weekend break in a lovely hotel. I came away feeling I had learned a lot and also with the confidence to pick up the cards and read for someone. I went home with great plans to continue, but somehow I didn't seem to take it any further at the time. Life got in the way.

One day I went to a Mind Body Spirit Fair, and seated at the tables were Tarot Readers, Palmists, Crystal Ball Readers and people known in the old days as fortune tellers. I went straight to the table of a young man who was an Angel Card Reader. His name was Michael and he spread the cards, after telling me to shuffle them. It is such a long time ago now that I can't remember what he told me. However, he stopped what he was doing at one point and said, "Why are you not sitting here instead of me?" The emotion welled up in me and I found the tears trickling down my face. "I wish I was, more than anything," I said. He told me to start giving free readings online and that would get me started. He might as well have told me to fly to the moon because I hadn't a clue about working in that way. Thanking him I didn't embarrass myself by saying that I was a dinosaur and I didn't have any idea how to work online. He gave me a little crystal and opening a box, and he gave me a Saint Cristopher medal to keep me safe on my journey through life. How kind he was! This young man certainly "walked his talk."

Discoveries on My Journey

Crystals

Back at my Angel Awareness class we learned about crystals and their healing powers. Until then, I had just looked on them as being beautiful stones. When we held them in our hands, we could feel their energy; they would go from cold to warm and sometimes pulse in our hands. I read books on crystals and discovered that they each have properties that are suitable for working with different illnesses. I had no idea then that they can also be programmed for sending out Love, Light, Peace, Healing and Protection for ourselves, others, the country, continent, Earth and beyond. Crystals are something that has fascinated me ever since.

As I have said earlier, this was a wonderful period in my life. I was finding out many things I had never known. I was also living in what I now know was a state of Grace. I saw the world as being a place of diversity in landscape and in what I considered beauty. Colours became brighter. I took time to look at landscapes, and I saw them as stunning, whereas before they were normal.

I became kinder to everyone and less judgemental, and I realised there was a connection between everyone and everything. It was as if I looked with a Spiritual view rather than a Human one; only later would I find out that we are all spirits having a human experience here on Earth. I began praying for our Earth, which I looked on as our temporary home. I saw it as a place we all need to take responsibility for, and we need to show respect for the planet we live on. We have been granted stewardship of what is basically a large sphere. As humans we plunder what lies beneath the surface, mining for minerals and removing oil and gas. When we have adverse weather conditions, earthquakes and volcanic eruptions, we ask, "Why does God let this happen to his people?" Do we ever stop to wonder if we have contributed to what has happened? We need to think about how we can leave this Earth in a more natural state and know that we have left it with enough resources for those who come here after us, whether human or animal. I realised that would be a mammoth task, but if we were all to do something, even something small, it could add up to a positive change for our lovely planet. We have become a throwaway society, unlike the previous generation who knew what it was like to make do and mend during wartime. Thinking of all this made me sad and I knew I had to think of the positive actions already taking place — recycling, using less plastic and removing plastic from our oceans, cleaner air policies, bringing negative practices to the attention of the public, planting more trees etc. All of these things and more are helping us to evolve as responsible human beings. A famous quote by Mahatma Gandhi is, "Be the change you wish to see in the world." I think we would do well to heed his words.

Aura Soma

During the time I was attending the Angel Awareness group, I heard of other workshops I could attend. I went to an Aura Soma afternoon. Aura Soma was first developed in 1983 by Vicky Wall, who was sixty-six years old and clinically blind. It is a system of bottles of liquid in jewel colours; they are a mixture of herbal oils, healing water and crystals. Aura Soma is used for the wellbeing of the person. It helps to calm and balance the energy system of our Mind, Body and Spirit. It strengthens and protects the aura which is the electro- magnetic energy field around our body. This helps us to reach our full potential in life. Meeting with a practitioner and choosing a few of the bottles from an extensive collection, people instinctively choose bottles that may reveal their gifts, challenges and opportunities. It was an interesting afternoon and it helped me to understand the benefits of colours, plants and crystals as a means of healing.

Colour Workshop

Later, my daughter-in-law told me of a Colour Workshop. She said she would take me to it as I didn't drive into Belfast. She decided we would go together, and I was pleased to have her company. I wore a beautiful rainbow silk scarf with hearts on it, a present she had kindly given to me. At the workshop in a hotel, I discovered that every colour has a vibration that affects our energy and the combined energy of the Earth. Colour affects everyone, whether we realise it or not. If we doubt this, we need only think of the colours we like and the fact that we usually have a favourite colour. There are colours we are drawn to and colours we do not like, and we don't have them in our clothing or surroundings at all. We sometimes use colour to explain how we are feeling. After a fright we are as 'white as a sheet.' We say we are 'green with envy,' 'feeling blue' when we are sad, 'seeing red' when we are angry etc. Colour can mean different things to different people. As a rough guide:

Red is the colour of passion.

Orange stimulates creativity.

Yellow increases fun in our lives.

Green is for balance and harmony.

Blue is for calmness, but it is also a good colour for communication.

Violet stimulates intuition.

Realising that colour can have a very powerful effect on our mood, I came to the conclusion that we need more colour in our lives. Sometimes we take the easy option and wear black, especially in winter. What better time is there to experiment with more cheerful colours?

Music

I thought about how sound affects us and I realised the healing power of music. It can stimulate us, and it can also relax us, and I made a mental note to play more of the music I love in my home. I realised that classical music has a high vibration that is good for the energy of the place where it is being played. I also know that music is good for the soul, and I decided I would play whatever made me feel happy. Instead of mindless television all the time, sometimes our home is filled with music. As a child I had wanted to be in the school choir, but the music teacher lined us up and we had to sing the scale. At eleven years old, we were nervous, and it didn't help when he called NEXT the minute I opened my mouth. I thought I couldn't sing and for years I only sang occasionally with the radio when no one was around. Now I sing as I go about my household chores, and I get great pleasure from it. Since I live in a detached house it has not affected my neighbours so far!

I remember one day my cousin, who is also consciously following her Spiritual Path, visited me. As soon as she walked into the room, she asked me why she could sense many people singing. I explained that I had been playing a CD of choir music a little while before she arrived. It was all the proof we needed of the effect music can have on our homes and indeed anywhere it has been played.

After that, I gave thought to the programmes I watched on T.V., and I began to understand that they brought good or bad energy into my home, depending on what I chose to watch. I have never been a fan of horror films or violence, so it wasn't too hard to monitor what is playing on television in our home. Some of our friends who are quite spiritual won't have a TV in their house, but if used properly I think it can educate us about our world and the people and animals in it. I am a great believer in all things in moderation.

Decluttering

I found myself decluttering our home and keeping that which was necessary or held great emotional value for us. Since everything is energy, it makes sense to only keep the things we love. Clearing out my wardrobe, I decided to let go of clothes I hadn't worn for a long time, things I hoped would fit me again if I lost weight. I found I had to learn to love myself as I was. These clothes were a reminder of failed diets. I could give the clothes to charity and let someone else get the benefit of them. If I were to lose weight, I could buy some new clothes and they would be a reward for getting the weight off.

Another thing I found it hard to part with was pictures. Art is something else that brings energy into our home and again beautiful art has a high vibration that is good for the surroundings as well as the soul. I visited a friend once who is a Spirit Artist; in other words, beautiful paintings are channelled through her. I don't know where it came from, but I told her that her work must be shown to the world. Her paintings are now being sold throughout the world and I feel that this is because their healing energy is needed wherever they go.

Around the time I found out about Reiki Healing and went on to do the First Degree in it, a Counselling course was advertised in the local paper. It was among the courses available at the College of Further Education, and it was just intended as a taster course. For some reason I felt drawn to it. I thought that if people came to me for healing and told me of their personal problems; it would help me to understand how I could help them. I signed up for a nine-month course and I enjoyed it so much that I studied counselling for three years. At the end of that time, I had an Advanced Diploma in Counselling. I had met some lovely people during the course, and we had helped each other by working through the troublesome times we had been through in our lives. We had quite a few laughs as well. Laughter can be very healing and it also attracts angels to us.

As part of the course, I had to have ten hours of counselling and I chose one of my former tutors to counsel me for this. By the time we had finished, I felt I knew myself very well. I realised that while he had been the most wonderful listening ear, I had been the one to work through my thoughts and feelings and I had learned to accept myself with his guidance. We had worked well together, and I knew that although I was not perfect I was going to be able to deal with whatever anyone had to tell me without judgement.

Attending the Spiritualist Church for a little while helped to satisfy my curiosity about Mediumship. I went to a few of the services and watched others giving healing to those in need. I told them a little about myself and my healing abilities, but they told me I would need to train with them for three years before I could work in hospitals etc. That seemed too long to wait before I could pass healing to others. Again, I was impatient. I was living around twenty miles from the church, and I didn't drive into the city of Belfast. Public transport was not convenient, and I didn't want my poor husband hanging around on cold winter nights if he were to drive me there, so I had to forget about training with them.

I attended a couple of psychic development classes, and I had gone to an open day where I had Angel Card readings. I enjoyed being in the company of people like myself. I attended a few demonstrations of Mediumship in different places, and although I prayed for those who needed comfort to receive evidence of Life after Death by getting messages from their loved ones who had passed over, I often had the medium give messages to me.

I found the whole thing fascinating. I felt the Mediums gave such detailed information and I was impressed that they were able to give evidence of

Life after Death. The messages brought so much comfort to people, and it seemed to take things a step further than those who counselled people suffering with grief and loss were able to do.

A part of me wished with all my heart that I had been able to do what they did, but I was afraid. I would have been happy if messages for others had just been shown to me in the mind's eye. Besides I had been told I was a healer and there had never been any mention of me being a Medium and passing on messages from the departed. Knowing this did not stop me reading all the books that were written by well-known Mediums and watching TV shows about them. Yes, I know there are some charlatans out there, but there are many caring, loving Mediums who have a great faith in God. They dedicate their lives to helping others. Some of the Mediums I have met do exorcisms — not something you would attempt without having God on your side, I would imagine.

Over the years my collection of books was growing, and I hit upon the idea of taking some of them to Kenny, the lovely Medium in Spain who had started me on my Spiritual Journey. I reached a point where I had read most of the books that were on sale in the Mind, Body, Spirit sections of the shops I went to. I am not saying I knew it all, but I stopped buying so many because the same information was often being repeated.

I enjoyed going to the Mind, Body, Spirit fairs. There were stalls selling everything — books, crystals, jewellery, lotions and potions for beauty and massage, candles, cards and wonderful crafts. It was possible to try out many of the holistic treatments. There were long queues for card readings. What interested me were the talks given by Spiritual people on many different topics. You see, I was a seeker on my Spiritual Journey back to the Source I thought of as God. That didn't mean I had closed my mind to other people's views; I was interested in listening to what they had to say, but I cherry-picked any information that fitted with my own views.

Someone mentioned a young woman who 'told fortunes' in the town where I lived, and she was of particular interest to me. I made an appointment to have my cards read and one afternoon I found myself sitting in her sunny kitchen. She was a nice-looking girl with a lively personality and I thought it only fair to tell her I was keeping something from her, but I would tell her what it was when we finished. After the reading which was pretty accurate, I dropped the bombshell. "I am your cousin," I said. She looked at me in surprise, "That is not what I expected — I thought you were another card reader" she said. She had gone to live in England as a child and we had never seen each other over the years. Her father and my mother were brother and sister. After that, we became firm friends — until she moved back to England and sadly we lost touch.

I had an e-mail from the lovely girl who had taught me at the Angel Awareness Class to say she was doing a workshop for Integrated Energy Therapy. I attended and found it had to do with healing the person by working on the information stored within the cells in their body. I completed the Basic Level and found it interesting. It was another chance to give and receive healing energy, and, as they say, every day is a school day — we are always learning something new. It was also nice to see the girl who had taught me so much about Angels and how to communicate with them.

Once I started sourcing Angel Awareness Classes, the people I met suggested other events. Those facilitating these events quite often had evenings of meditation, often at their homes, but sometimes in hotels or halls. That was how I met some wonderful teachers who furthered my learning about Angels and Healing. I attended meditations with a lovely couple in Belfast for a while. To say the meditations were out of this world would be putting it mildly. During this time, I saw glimpses of such beauty it reduced me to tears. I was privileged to see the wonderful faces of Angels — amazing gardens and beautiful domed buildings, like cathedrals. These were just a few of the things I saw in my semi-conscious state. It all seemed like it was happening in a dream but a dream I would remember forever.

I heard of a Crystal Workshop in the Isle of Man, and I was so keen to attend that I travelled alone, which was unusual for me. I enjoyed every moment of the course which was hosted in a lovely rural setting in five-star accommodation. I was fascinated by the colourful array of crystals that adorned the room the workshop was being held in, but more than that the energy was protective and calm. The others attending the workshop couldn't have been a more caring group, fitting together to work with the crystals as if they had been born to be together at that moment in time. We used the crystals to clear our auras, give reflexology and send healing to others, the Earth and the Planets. How amazing it was that I had been able to be a part of all of this. I felt humble and yet I felt proud at the same time. I didn't know when I said goodbye to Raye, the lady running the course that I would soon be in need of her help.

I returned home and life went back to normal. I had my counselling exams and, in the lead up to them, I became stressed. I don't know whether that sparked off something in me. I became weepy and a bit down just before Christmas and my energy suffered. Although I had passed every exam I sat, I knew something was wrong with me. I continued saying my prayers but my dreams were not good. I gave myself Reiki Healing treatments but still my dark mood continued. There was nothing else for it; I knew I had to seek help.

I got in touch with the girl who had been my teacher for the Angel Awareness classes. Although she lived twenty miles away, she said she would come to see me. After talking together for a while, she agreed that my energy was low. Taking a clear quartz crystal, she swept it through my aura. Instantly, I began to feel a little better. I tried to give her money, which she did not want to accept. In the end she agreed, provided she could give it to the animal charity she supported. How lovely of her and how kind she was.

I tried to pick myself up, but again I just felt I didn't have the energy. I got in touch with Raye, the lady from the crystal course in the Isle of Man. She said, "You and your husband must get on a plane and come to spend New Year with my husband and I." I protested that it wouldn't be fair to come during the Christmas Holidays. She told me to come and she would do everything she could to help me. I talked to my husband and we booked a flight to Liverpool where she and her husband met us at the airport. Their kindness knew no limits and for the few days we stayed with them they both gave me Reiki Healing. We went for walks through the fields and the woods in the frost and a light coating of snow. This was to make me feel grounded. We dined on healthy food, drank a little wine and I began to feel much better. She brought her extensive crystal collection to the kitchen table, and we held and admired the crystals and the energy was wonderful.

Raye was a teacher of teachers for many of the holistic therapies and I knew I was in good hands. When I admired the artwork in the house, she explained she was a Spirit Artist which meant that she was being guided as she was drawing or painting. She offered to draw a picture of my guide or angel but only if I gave my permission and she also sought the permission of my guide or angel. I was fascinated that this was possible, and I couldn't wait to watch her working. She took a large drawing pad, and I realised she was looking at me and not the paper as the pencil in her hand flew over the page, the lines of a beautiful Angel becoming visible. As she worked, she gave me a reading of wonderful advice from my angel. I was overcome with emotion when I saw the beautiful drawing. She told me I was to colour it in when I returned home.

What an amazing human being! Her husband had been lovely to us also. I went home feeling we had made two wonderful friends and I also knew I was so much stronger than when I arrived.

We bought one of her paintings which she posted

to us, and we could hardly wait for its arrival when we got home. When it arrived, we chose the best place in our home to hang it. We still have that painting, and, after my husband Daniel, it is the first thing I would save if there was a fire. It is a painting of mystery, but I think it is of the circle of life. Over a period of a few years, we went on to buy another four of her spiritual paintings. They bring a special energy to our home. We visited the couple in Wales, and they came to see us in Northern Ireland a few times. I did my Reiki Master attunement with Raye on one of her visits. Later she came to Ireland and attended an Angel Card Reading Course with me. It was something I had been longing to do for a long time. We had a lot of fun together but now we keep in touch about once a year, and, strange as it may sound, I also see her in my dreams from time to time.

Dreams

Dreams are something else we need to focus on when we are consciously following our Spiritual Path because information can be given to us in this way. It is wise to invest in a decent dream book to help us to interpret what we are seeing. My first strange dream was of looking down upon a pond and seeing a goldfish swimming for quite a long time. The fish is a symbol of Christianity. I later went on to open the pink ribbon on the iron gates of a neglected garden. Was I opening the gates to the possibilities within myself? As the years have passed, I have been shown the garden in its progression. At one time I dreamt of the choice I had to make between a beautifully furnished cottage and an empty castle. I chose the cottage, but I was then shown the castle furnished in all its splendour. I knew that I had chosen the one I was comfortable with, but if I was prepared to get out of my comfort zone and push myself, I could have the castle. I took this dream to mean if I put more effort into self-actualizing I could be more than I had first envisaged. One of my Spiritual

Teachers told me that we are like sparkling diamonds that have gathered the dust of a lifetime and in order to shine we must realise that and begin polishing the beautiful diamonds that we are.

Another dream I have often is of Christmas. I am working so hard with all the preparations that I forget to put up the Christmas tree. Does this mean that I am so busy with day-to-day things that I forget to have fun in my life? Psychotherapists use dreams as a way of understanding their clients' problems, and they would probably say it is our subconscious working to help us make sense of our lives. However, I feel it is the way the Angels are helping me by giving me information while I sleep. I am not the only one this happens to. It is said that we all dream every night whether we remember it or not. They never stop trying to help us. Feeling tired one day, I remember telling my mother and stepfather that someone takes me away in my sleep and makes me work hard. They thought it was hilarious. My stepfather said, "I wish they would bring you here to weed the garden for us!" Early in my journey I was told to keep a note pad by the bed for the purpose of writing down my dreams. It is something we must do on waking because if we leave it until later, we may not remember the dream or it may not be so clear.

Angel Meditations with Mary

I think about the times in my life when I have prayed for help and guidance and I can see that although it may take a little time, my prayers have always been answered. This may not be in the way I expected or indeed hoped for but usually it has been for my highest and greatest good. I was meant to meet Raye, the Crystal lady in the Isle of Man. She is a wonderful healer, and she has helped me on many occasions, not only with my own healing but also by sending Reiki to others when I have requested it. She is one of the most fun, down-to-earth people I have ever met. We lived quite a distance apart, both of us had busy lives and I missed her, but I also realised that sometimes people come into our lives to assist with the lessons we need to learn and sometimes they learn from us. After our time together we get on with our lives, and that is how it is meant to be. It was great knowing that the Angels were teaching me all the time, but I longed for a human mentor, someone who would be able to answer my questions and understand me because their Spiritual Path was similar to mine. When my daughter-in-law asked me if I would like to join her for an Angel Day in Belfast I had no idea my prayers were about to be answered.

I joined my daughter-in-law, Jill, and her lovely friend, Nicola, in Belfast Castle. I felt fortunate to be in the lovely castle set amongst the trees on Cave Hill. Admiring the amazing views of the city, I didn't know I was about to meet the Spiritual teacher I had asked for. Her name was Mary, and when she entered the room, where a large number of woman and a few men were assembled, she explained that we were going to have a day of meditation dedicated to the Angels. She spoke softly of Angels and Ascended Masters and the energy in the room was one of peace and joy. It felt clear and pure as a sparkling silver stream. I felt privileged to be there.

I was so impressed by her lovely gentle ways that I began attending her workshops about once a month, although she lived a long distance away. God Bless my husband, he drove me to her home and collected me afterwards. She had a rented cottage on a private estate, and it was a joy to visit. The energy was uplifting the moment you walked through the door. She lived alone and her home was adorned with all the things she loved. The colours of the interior were beautiful; soft shades of the rainbow were all around. The marble mantelpiece was a shelf for the most amazing crystals as were the window-sills. Each group of crystals was dedicated to healing. Bookshelves held spiritual books and plants. The walls were covered in pictures of the Ascended Masters and the cushions and throws used for our comfort during meditation were from India. I have always been interested in interior design but the atmosphere in the cottage went beyond the choosing of beautiful things. There was a peace and harmony that I hadn't known outside of a visit to a church.

Mary suited her surroundings. She was like an Angel herself. Dressed in clothes of pastel colours and wearing little pieces of crystal jewellery she was the picture of femininity and grace. When she moved, she glided. It was as if her feet never touched the floor. Yet this was a woman, who was grounded, she worked in hospitals with cancer patients. The people attending the workshops were graceful and softly spoken and at first I wondered what they would think of me. Physically I was larger than average, and quietness was not a virtue I possessed. I needn't have worried; they were all lovely to me.

We meditated, learned about the Ascended Masters, Angels, Archangels and the higher realms. We learned about Sacred Geometry and Crystals and again I was reminded of the importance of healing energy. I think most of all I witnessed God's Grace in action by studying Mary herself. She was an example to all of us. I left her home those days on a high. I didn't want to talk afterwards; I just wanted to allow everything I had learned to settle in to my mind. My husband concentrated on the road ahead, he seemed to accept my need for peace and quiet on the drive home. At times like that I knew how much I loved and appreciated the wonderful life-partner by my side.

Daniel and I had travelled a lot during our life together. As well as our travels on board ships when were first married, we had taken holidays in the Greek Islands, Canary Islands, Malta and also around the U.K. We had visited the Gambia, Cuba and Hawaii before going to live in Spain, and, since our return from Spain, we had holidays in Egypt and India. I firmly believe our energy was needed in those places at that time. Although he didn't join me for any of the workshops, I felt deeply honoured to have someone I loved and who loved me, walking with me on my Spiritual Journey.

Glastonbury

Quite soon after our return from living in Spain our son, Gary, and his partner, Natalie, moved to England. Gary had been 'head-hunted' for a job there, and he felt it was too good an opportunity to miss. They rented out their property in Northern Ireland and with their car heavily laden with their suitcases, two dogs and three cats; they set off for the south of England. Renting a house gave them time to search for a suitable property, which they found quite quickly. As soon as they were settled Daniel and I wasted no time in spending our holidays with them. I always left them in tears, but it was worth it just to have seen them again.

Although they lived in Dorset, we flew into Bristol airport and stopped in Glastonbury on our way down to the south of England. It is the most beautiful little town, and it was wonderful to walk around in the amazing energy there. Glastonbury is the Heart chakra of the planet. The Michael and Mary Ley lines pass through it and the energy as I said is beautiful. One day I was asleep in the car on the way to Glastonbury from Bristol and just as I was about to wake up, I saw what I can only describe as electricity pylons, but they looked as if they were made from light. I couldn't see them when I woke up properly so I can only assume I was being made aware of the healing energy being conveyed to or from the area.

Glastonbury Tor is the first landmark you see as you arrive. It is a green grassy mound with St. Michael's Tower at the top. The tower is the remainder of a 14th century Church that was built to replace an earlier one. It is thought that Jesus once visited the area with his uncle, Joseph of Arimathea. (I read later that Joseph of Arimathea was a merchant who may have visited England to buy tin from the tin mines in Cornwall.) This story is written about in a poem by William Blake which later became the hymn 'Jerusalem.'

Glastonbury Tor is thought to be the Isle of Avalon in the legend of King Arthur. Known as one of the most Spiritual sites in England, it is visited by thousands every year.

At the foot of the Tor is Chalice Wells. The natural spring is set in beautiful gardens and is owned and maintained by the Chalice Well Trust. According to Christian Mythology, the well marks the spot where Joseph of Arimathea placed the Chalice that had caught the drops of Christ's blood at the crucifixion, thus linking the well to the Holy Grail. In the gardens there is a tree known as the Glastonbury Thorn; it is usual for it to bloom twice a year, one of those times being at Christmas. The tree is said to have grown after Joseph of Arimathea drove his staff into the ground. When we visited, we were overwhelmed by the peace and beauty of the place. The water, which is slightly red in colour, is said to have healing qualities and is free for all who wish to partake of it. We spent some time there in contemplation, meditation and prayer.

With reluctance, we left the gardens and we moved on to visit Glastonbury Abbey. The Abbey is thought to be the earliest Christian foundation in Britain and Christian legend claims that in the 1st century it was founded by Joseph of Arimathea. The Abbey is associated with the legend of King Arthur and Avalon. In the 12th century the monks are alleged to have discovered the tomb of King Arthur and Queen Guinevere. It was summer when we first visited and we spent a pleasant couple of hours there. The peaceful energy would have been hard to resist.

For me there is no doubt that Glastonbury is a mystical place. I discovered while researching it that although I have talked only of the Christian history, Pagans from all over the world visit Glastonbury.

The wonderful little town is situated a few miles from where the music festival is held. I was in my element walking around it. The shops sell everything from the 'New Age', crystals, books and clothing to flowers, fruit, vegetables, bread and cakes. We were fortunate to be able to sample the food while we were there, as the town offers a selection of little restaurants and cafes, some with healthy eating options as one would expect. A favourite of ours was an old English tearoom.

Needless to say, we loved Glastonbury so much we returned to it many times. My daughter-in-law used to say, "Why don't you go back to Glastonbury and top up your energy?" when we had stayed with her for a few days. I always felt as though my batteries had been recharged after a visit to Glastonbury.

We also visited Stonehenge. It was somewhere I had always wanted to see, and the massive monoliths did not disappoint. At the time we visited, it was surrounded by a wire fence which meant we joined the many people who were walking around it in an anti-clockwise direction. We met a girl walking in the opposite direction and suddenly I realised she was right in doing so. She was following the same path as the sun — she was walking clockwise! It was a sharp reminder to me to do what you feel is right regardless of what others might think or do.

Avebury Stone Circles in Wiltshire was a place we

visited more than once. We were fortunate that Gary and Natalie were living in Dorset, because of all the wonderful sights we had seen and experiences we'd had when we visited them.

Sometimes we need to remind ourselves of the lovely places we can visit without travelling very far. Daniel and I are proud of the beautiful scenery we have in the north and south of Ireland. We had a couple of lovely weekends holidaying in Donegal in the Northwest of Ireland. Angel workshops were held in a hotel. They had such a special energy and my soul was refreshed. It was good to be with people who were like me, who believe in the power of Angels. They sent out love, light and healing wherever they went, and they prayed that the Earth might become a better place because of it. During our holidays in Donegal, I discovered somewhere I would like to have as my final resting place on this Earth. When we went there on holiday with the family, we used to walk through a beautiful peaceful green valley to a waterfall. I told them on one visit that I would like to have my ashes scattered there, that way I would remain free and not be confined to a grave. I knew that my soul would return to the place from whence it came, but it gave me comfort to think that my body in the form of ashes would nourish the lovely valley I had chosen. How did the family take my announcement? They took it without comment because Daniel and I have never tried to hide the fact that one day we shall leave the Earth. Dying is as natural as living.

Return to Spain

I missed living in Spain, but there was no question of us returning on a permanent basis; we had come back to Northern Ireland and that was that. Spain was to be reserved for holidays and November and February were good times to go — it shortened the winter for us. We had left good friends there, and it was great to see them from time to time. They looked forward to our visits also.

I don't know what happened to me but my energy became low, and I felt unwell. Nothing seemed to lift me out of the mood I had got into, and tiredness had become part of everyday life. Daniel was working, having been asked to go back to work for his old firm on our return from living in Spain. We had missed our holiday in November because it wasn't convenient for him to take time off work. He came home one day, and I said, "My mental health is going the wrong way and if I am not careful I will end up in a hospital." He asked me what he could do to help me, and I said, "I need to get away, I need the sun."

I had suffered from Seasonal Affected Disorder before I had gone to live in Spain, and I knew it was back. It was wintertime, with grey skies and rain every day, and I couldn't stand it any longer. I knew that in February the temperatures were not high in Spain, but the skies were blue and the sun shone and I hoped that would be enough to make me well.

Luckily, I am married to a wonderful man, and he knew I was at my lowest ebb. He said, "Right, I will rent a place in Spain for you for a month and since I have to work here, I will visit you every other weekend." I didn't want to go and live on my own — I am not that adventurous — but I knew I would have to do it. It was my last chance of becoming well; otherwise I would have had to see my GP to ask for anti-depressants. So it was that I found myself packing a case with enough clothes for a month while my husband booked our flights and hotel for a week. I was crying constantly in the privacy of my meditation room without knowing why.

We booked into our usual hotel and every day we looked for somewhere for me to stay. I needed to feel safe since I would be alone. A part of me knew I was in no fit state to be left alone, and I would hate to be by myself when it was time for him to go home. I couldn't burden my friends by going to stay with them in my state of mind. We visited our friends, Chris and Dave, and we told them I wasn't well, and

I needed an apartment to rent for a little while. Later, Chris telephoned to say her Spanish teacher had the perfect apartment, and she would be prepared to rent it to us. It was in a coastal town near Benidorm and after seeing it and knowing the owner lived close by, we decided it was what I needed.

We left the hotel and moved in straight away. It was a beautiful apartment near the beach — simply decorated with beautiful paintings on the walls and a peaceful energy. We shopped for my food for the next month. Next day, it was time for Daniel to leave. I was heartbroken — how would I survive on my own? After he left, my friend Chris phoned to see if I was ok, and, at that point, I felt anything but ok. I told her I didn't know if I was going to be strong enough to get through this time alone. She told me if I wanted to go home, she and Dave would book a flight for me and take me to the airport. That was not what I wanted; it would not have solved anything. She told me that she was there for me if I needed to talk and that she and Dave would visit and we would go out for dinner often if I stayed. I knew then that I had two wonderful friends to support me no matter what happened. I made up my mind to stay and see it through.

If I am being honest, I had also felt a certain relief when Daniel left. I had been trying not to cry in front of him and now I would be able to let the tears flow.

Why was I crying? To this day I don't know the answer to that. All I know is that healers are sensitive and sometimes on the Spiritual journey we have what is known as 'clearing' to do. We pick up the feelings and emotions of not only ourselves but others also as we go through life, and sometimes it is important to allow ourselves time to let go of those emotions and become renewed and revitalized.

If I had known then what I know now, I would have gone to a retreat — a place where I would have had someone to care for my basic needs and give me a little counselling while I spent time praying, meditating, exercising and becoming well. Instead, I had to find my own way. It began with releasing some of that emotion through accepting that I was not feeling well and that it was ok to feel sad and cry. Next morning, I went out to the little balcony and took a seat in the sunshine. What happened next is hard to explain. It was as if a ripple of energy went through me from my head to my feet. I felt that I was loved and understood by a force greater than myself. I don't know how long I sat there but there was a sense of knowing everything was going to be alright. I made plans for how I would spend my time in Spain to get the most out of it.

I had brought a notebook with me, and I decided to keep a journal of my thoughts, feelings and how I had spent my days. Next, I decided I would put myself on a healthy diet with plenty of fruit and vegetables, fish and chicken. I knew gluten was not agreeing with me and my normal intake of bread was not doing me any favours. I decided to keep bread and the sweet treats I was so fond of to a minimum. I suppose I was thinking healthy body, healthy mind. I would take better care of myself. I started by exfoliating my skin and applying lots of moisturiser after my shower. I brushed my hair until it shone and every day and I applied a little make up even if I didn't feel like it. Soon, I was able to look at myself in the mirror again. Exercise was something I hadn't been getting enough of at home in the winter months. Housework and shopping were not enough to keep me healthy and fit. I was in a beautiful part of the world with a long promenade and sunshine, so there was no excuse for not walking. Every day I saw others exercising — running, walking and doing yoga from dawn until dusk. It gave me the incentive to plan my way back to health. I walked further and further on the long promenade every morning and also later in the afternoon, and I could feel myself getting fitter all the time.

It was during one of my walks into the town that I discovered a little café with a sign outside saying, 'Spirit Café, everyone welcome.' Hopefully I looked more confident than I felt when I walked inside.

There were a lot of ladies and a couple of men sitting at various tables having tea. Someone said, "Come and join us," and before I knew it I was part of the group and not just an onlooker. One of the ladies explained that they met there twice a week. They discussed all things Spiritual, and they gave each other healing if it was requested. I knew I was in the right place. I felt someone had just entered and I could sense a person staring at me. I looked up and there stood Kenny, the man who had started me on my Spiritual Journey. The group went silent, and they looked on with great interest when he walked over to me and put his arms around me. "Where is Daniel?" he asked. "He has left me here to sort myself out," I replied. The group resumed their chat, and I explained how I was feeling. Bless Kenny, he gave me some healing and assured me I would be alright.

Although the people came from many different countries in Europe, they all spoke English, and when Kenny talked, they hung onto his every word. If someone had told me he was a modern-day version of a sage, I would have believed them. Of all the lovely ladies there, I noticed one lady who was very serene and quite beautiful. Around her neck was a turquoise scarf and it was as if I was drinking in the colour. She was much quieter than the others, but she did not escape my attention. Why she was of interest to me, I don't know. I didn't get to know her that day, but one day she sat beside me, and we got talking. She was Norwegian and her name was Anne-Lise. After finding out she was alone and had rented an apartment for the winter months, I asked her if she was ever lonely. She laughed and said, "Sometimes I miss my family a little, but each day I walk, and, in my mind, I send love to everyone I meet. I smile at everyone and often they smile back at me. I sit at the little cafes in the sun and if people talk to me, I talk to them and so I am not lonely." As I got to know her, I knew I had a lot to learn from this woman. She felt complete within herself, and she was happy with her life. She would have liked a male partner to share her life, but if the right person did not come along, that was ok. She was grateful for everything she had and the opportunity to spend the cold Norwegian winter in sunny Spain. As we talked together, we formed a friendship that is ongoing many years later.

Our first meal together was at a Chinese restaurant, and that evening I was happy I had made a new friend. It came as no surprise when she told me that she was a healer. She had such a calm, gentle way about her; she was the kind of person who made you feel well just by being in her company. We arranged to meet for lunch at a little Italian restaurant soon after. We ordered a pizza, salad and wine, and, as she began eating, she said "What have you done to me?"

I was startled by this, and I said, "What do you mean?" She replied, "I almost did not come for lunch today because I have pains in my hands sometimes, and they were really bad today. I thought I might not be able to hold the knife and fork. Now I am feeling ok, have you done something?" I explained that I too am a healer and although I had not consciously sent healing to her; perhaps it was flowing through me anyway. I thanked God for the healing because I am just an ordinary woman, and without Him channelling the healing through me this little miracle would not have happened. I was happy Anne-Lise felt so much better, and since I have known her, she has prayed for me and, at times, given me wonderful healing as well as sending it to my family and friends when I have requested it.

I thought back to one time when I was talking to Kenny and I asked him why did I feel bad sometimes — why did my son have a motorbike accident, why had I lost my credit cards? I was doing my best now I had committed to being a healer and I thought my life would be filled with only good things. He looked at me quite seriously and said, "Healers need to understand how it is for others, but how can they know if they are never ill or only good things happen to them?" I understood then that I would not have a free pass for the rest of my life. I felt sure the Angels must have been laughing because I had been allowing my ego to get in the way of common sense.

Our friends Chris and Dave were as good as their word. On Mondays, Chris had a Spanish lesson with my landlady and afterward she and Dave came and took me out for a Chinese meal. I was not used to living alone, and I was so grateful for their company. They couldn't have been kinder at a time when I needed it most. They brought me a DVD player and some DVDs of musicals and movies with a happy vibe. Although they lived about thirty minutes' drive from me, they called for me when they were having a day out. We went to the Jalon Valley to purchase wine from the bodegas. We stocked up on oranges there also. We went to Guadalest, a lovely old Spanish village in the hills, and one of my favourite places in the entire world. The little shops there are wonderful. Lunches on our days out were special. Usually, we dined on typically Spanish cuisine, and I quite often insisted on paying because, as I explained to Chris, money was not something I was short of, but good friends are harder to find. Chris was a great cook, and she always got her own back by having Daniel and I to their home for Tapas or dinner.

After the sadness I suffered the first week, my life fell into a little pattern. I showered, had breakfast and then walked into the shopping area of the town to purchase anything I needed. On my return to the apartment, I did a little housework and then took a walk along the promenade; stopping for coffee outside the hotel and watching the world go by. The sun and the beautiful sea view were doing their work and I was improving every day. Lunch was a tuna or cheese salad back at the apartment. Meditation and reading took up a good part of the afternoon. A couple of days a week, I joined the group at the Spirit café, and I saw Chris and Dave at least twice a week for lunch or dinner. In the early evenings, just before the sun set, I walked the length of the promenade again and I telephoned family in the evenings as I knew they were concerned about me being alone. I remember telling them that God was right to place Eve on the Earth with Adam as loneliness is hard to cope with. I vowed that I would take more notice of people who were on their own and speak to them if I met them even if it was just to say hello. Already I was learning to think of others. My enforced loneliness was of my own doing, some people didn't have a choice.

I didn't realise it at the time but being alone was teaching me so much. I started noticing things that I would have been oblivious to before. In the apartment, I placed my chair at the table with a view from the window. Sitting down for my evening meal, I asked God and the Angels for inner peace. I was rewarded with the most amazing sunset. The sky was lit with the glorious colours of orange and red. The distant mountain, Puig Compana, was silhouetted in inky black. Mentally I praised God for the revelation of the glory I saw before me.

Next morning, a little sparrow landed on my window ledge to eat something he had brought with him; as he moved closer to the edge, I knew that I also needed to take a few risks in life. I watched him for some time, grateful for his being there. I felt the same as I looked at a pigeon on my balcony the following day; its feathers shone with iridescent colours in the sunlight, whereas before I would have described them as grey. One night when I was feeling lonely and emotional, a sound at the window attracted my attention, I looked up and a beautiful white dove hovered for a little while before flying skywards. It reminded me of the Holy Spirit and God's promise, 'I will never leave you or forsake you, I am with you always.' Even though I was living alone, He had sent the Comforter to show me I was never really alone. The beauty of these birds had taught me so much, and, somehow, I felt they were bringing messages from the Angels. Realising I was beginning to appreciate nature again; I knew I was becoming well.

My experience with the birds reminded me that Angels are with us from before our soul comes to the Earth until we are taken home, when our physical body dies. They wait for us to ask for their help. This is something we need to ask for because they are not allowed to interfere with our freedom of choice.

One day, when I was walking in the town, I went into a shop and bought myself a box of paints, canvas and instructions for painting a picture. I hadn't painted since I was at school, so I surprised myself. Looking back, it was a way of bringing my creativity out. We have been put on this Earth to create; it is God's intention for us, and I now know if we find something we enjoy doing, it makes us feel happier. It is quite often when we are absorbed in something that we have our best ideas. Who puts those ideas in our head?

Some people say they can't draw, but I read somewhere that if we can write we can draw. The alphabet contains all of the strokes we will ever make with a pencil while drawing a picture. Practice is what makes us better at art, at everything really. There are so many forms of creativity — writing, music, dancing, singing, cooking, needlework, jewellery making etc. The angels encourage us to do whatever makes our heart sing.

Daniel, bless him, listened to my day's events every night on the phone. We are a close couple and I missed him very much. He told me he knew this was a part of my journey I needed to be alone for, but I was glad when I had been there eleven days and he was due to come for a visit. He found me looking and behaving a lot better than when he had left me. My routine, the one I had put in place for myself was non-existent over the weekend and we did whatever he suggested since he was there for a short time. He had been so patient and kind with me and I wanted him to see how much I had improved. And I wanted to make sure he enjoyed the weekend. He was pale after being at home and working every day, and, as I looked at him, I knew how much this man loved me. I knew the sacrifices he had made for me. I could never have had a better life partner. I went along with everything he wanted to do that weekend, but it also made me think of how often I gave my power away and let others decide for me. I thought of the kindness of people, but I realised that sometimes we need to make our own choices; otherwise we lose confidence in ourselves and our ability to know what is best for us. I learned during my time there that sometimes it is OK to say no.

After Daniel left, I knew I had only a fortnight left in Spain and the real work I needed to do on myself would have to begin. My routine was put back in place, and I thought how much better my life was for it. I was growing stronger and fitter with all the walking I was doing. I had lost a little weight and it suited me. Being in the company of friends taught me the great effect laughter has on our wellbeing. Someone once said, "A day without laughter is a day wasted." I believe they were absolutely right. With a joyful heart, I found it was time to invoke the help of the Angels to assess myself as a person in order to know what changes I had to make before my return. I prayed to God and I asked the Angels to help me make sense of my life up to that point.

A Time of Reckoning

I had a happy childhood, eldest of seven children, sometimes living in the country, sometimes in the town. When I was fourteen years-old, I lived in America for six months with my aunt and uncle. At sixteen, I shared an apartment with two other girls, and I had not done a bad job of looking after myself during that time. When I was eighteen, I had got married to a man who would be in and out of my life for the next twelve years because he went to sea. I had a couple of trips with him on oil tankers, and then we had two lovely sons and I spent my life focusing on them. I think sometimes we forget that once you are a mother, you are a mother for life. Daniel had been the main bread winner for all of those years, but he had also been working abroad for quite a lot of that time. I had needed to be a strong woman and I felt I had done a good job of bringing up our boys; they were decent human beings with good jobs and to me they are my greatest achievement in life. I had a husband I loved, and he loved me, of that I was in no doubt.

I had worked in various jobs over the course of my life and gained experience of people and their lives during that time. Most of those jobs had involved working with others and in the service of people. Retail, hospitality and tour guiding, which had been very similar to teaching had left me with a sense of achievement. All of these things had been the focus of my working life. Thinking of this, I was reminded of the fact that, being the eldest of seven children, I had helped my mother to rear my brothers and sisters when I was young. Looking after my own children had been paramount for a lot of years. Was that what I had been put on this Earth for? Was it my life purpose to look after others? In doing this had I forgotten about myself as we all do from time to time? The soul searching went on.

I continued to think about my life and the changes that had come to pass since I had been told I was a healer. My life path had not always been easy, but there had been some wonderful interludes as well. We could all say the same thing; we are on a roller coaster ride with highs and lows. What a privilege to be on our beautiful Earth, being able to rise every morning to the hope of a new dawn. We have another chance to write or rewrite the script for our lives. Sometimes I wondered what life would have been like if I had not discovered I was on my Spiritual Journey. Did I ever regret finding out that there is more to life than we first realise? Was I happy with my Life Purpose? This trip, with the time being spent mainly on my own gave me time to ponder all of these things and more.

I had married at a young age, and I hadn't given myself a chance to discover much about who I was, but this time alone had given me that chance. At this point the phrases "know thyself" and "to thine own self be true" sprung to mind. I realised that sometimes we can be very hard on ourselves by being judgemental. We judge and berate ourselves in a way we wouldn't dream of doing with a friend. Sometimes, it would be nice to stop and be a friend to ourselves. If we could view ourselves in the same way the Angels do, our lives would be very different. They look upon us with love and understanding, seeing the beauty of the soul within us. We judge ourselves and also others and sometimes see only what we think of as "wrong" when there is so much to appreciate. An example of this is when we stand in front of a mirror and focus on the parts we don't like about ourselves, while neglecting all the wonderful features we have been gifted with. I remember being critical of someone when I was young, and my father looked at me sternly and said, "People have to live; you do not know what they are going through." He was absolutely right; we should have compassion for others and try to help them if possible. We should also extend that compassion to ourselves.

I came to the conclusion that I should give the same love to myself as I did to others. It is by loving ourselves that we understand the true meaning of love in all its complexities. We are better placed to pass that love and understanding on after we have experienced it ourselves.

I had been extremely fortunate to have travelled all over the world with my husband, seeing lands I had never envisaged visiting. I realised we had accrued a lifetime of memories together. Had all of these life experiences equipped me to work as a healer, showing compassion to others? I think that everything I had been and seen and done, whether I felt it was good or bad at the time led up to that moment in my life. I had been well educated in the University of Life. Now I understood why I had needed to get away from everything that was familiar to me — I had needed time alone to think. When Daniel returned to take me home, I was sad to leave my old friends, Chris, Dave and Kenny, and my new friends at the Spirit Café, especially Anne-Lise. It was time to go, however; I had work to do, and I couldn't wait to see my family again especially now that I was feeling better. I slotted back into my life — older and wiser. I had learned to be grateful for everything I was and everything I had. Something else I realised was that if I was to work with others needing healing, I needed to have more fun in my life. My holiday alone had also reminded me that I missed Spain. I talked to Daniel and we decided we would try to spend the month of February every year in Spain.

When the boys were in their teens, we had moved to the house where I had a Bed and Breakfast for a number of years. They were in their twenties when Daniel and I moved to Spain for three years. Missing family and especially our sons we had returned home to Northern Ireland. Foolishly, I had imagined our sons needed us, as they had come out of long-term relationships. In truth, both of them were happy with new partners soon after. At first, I missed the boys' former partners; grief does not just follow someone dying I discovered. The girls had been such a part of our lives before we went to live in Spain, and, suddenly, I felt I should put away any photographs that included them so that it would not upset the new girls we had welcomed into our family. It was not just the boys' ex-partners we missed in the beginning; we also missed their families. We had grown close to them: we were great friends and we had socialised together before we went to live in Spain. It was as if we had to put our memories of all those happy times away with the photograph albums.

There was no question of us keeping in touch. In

order for everyone to move on we just had to go our separate ways. It would not have been fair to any of the girls, otherwise. Like most parents, all we wanted for our sons was their happiness and they had found that happiness with the new girls.

Returning to Northern Ireland after living in Spain for three years, we moved into the house we had bought with our youngest son, Gary. His brother Alan had also moved in after the breakup of his relationship. So, for a few months, we were a family again until Alan moved out and got a home of his own, which he shared quite soon after with his girlfriend, Jill. It had always been our intention to find a home of our own and we bought the bungalow I mentioned earlier. It was lovely being close to family again and catching up with all their news. Soon we had some news of our own! We were to become grandparents. Alan and his girlfriend Jill were expecting their first son. In the four years that followed they had another little boy and four years later a little girl.

During this time Gary and his girlfriend, Natalie, had moved to England, and, soon after, they had a little son and then a daughter. Within the space of nine years, we had become grandparents to five lovely grandchildren. At first, I must admit I thought it was great that my sons were grown up — no more worries, time for Daniel and me. I didn't know if I felt ready to be a grandmother. Soon I fell in love with the new little people who had come into our lives and now we cannot imagine life without them. They bring so much joy into everyday things and they keep us young.

Daniel and I moved to a beautiful house by the coast, where we decorated a room for meditation. The grandchildren call it my quiet room and are respectful of it when they visit. I spend time in it almost every night. Sometimes, my mind goes back through the years to the wonderful memories I have of the people who have left this world and taken the journey home as we will all do one day. I bless their Souls and I thank them for the love and kindness they have shown to others while they were on the Earth. While talking to Kenny, the lovely man who made me aware of my Life Purpose, one day I complained that the people of wisdom were all leaving my life. He told me it is now my turn to be a woman of wisdom for others; hopefully, with the assistance of the angels, I shall do my best to pass on their guidance to anyone who asks for help.

Meantime, I pray and send healing to anyone who needs it and to the Earth. I give thanks to God the father, my Lord Jesus Christ and the Holy Spirit, my Guides and Angels, the beloved Archangels and wonderful Guardian Angels and to all those in Spirit who help us here on the Earth. I listen to music as I write and, sometimes, I paint. I light a candle and call upon my beloved Angels, they never let me down. I feel them around me; their gentle energy is such a comfort. My life has been blessed with all the things I wish for every man woman and child on the Earth — love and light, peace and healing, beauty and joy, strength and abundance and, most of all, the wisdom of God. Not only do I have my guardian Angel but a host of other Angels when I call upon them. I also have Archangel Michael with his beautiful blue cloak of protection to call upon if I am ever afraid. Am I special? The answer is, in the Heavens we are all looked upon as being special. I am no different to anyone else. I feel we all have a Life Purpose, a reason for being on Earth. The Angels are there for all of us to ease our path on this Earth until we finally return to our Creator. Let's start by thanking them for everything they do and call on them when we need their help for ourselves or others.

Is my life a bed of roses? The answer is: of course not. I have great days when everything seems as I would wish it, but there are also days when I feel life is testing me. Those are days when I have learnt to be grateful for the lessons I have been taught. I wish everyone who reads this book the contentment I now feel while following my Spiritual Path, whether it happens to be rough or smooth. I remember being asked during my counselling class if I could turn back the clock ten years, would I? My answer then was, "No, I would not swap the wisdom I have gained for anything." I still feel the same now as I did then.

Perhaps, like me you have been fortunate enough to know what the purpose of your life on the Earth is. If not, the clues may lie in the life you have already lived. What did you want to be when you were a child, before life got in the way? I have told my grandchildren if they choose a career they love, it will seem as if they never have to work a day in their lives and they shall look forward to every new day. It is never too late to ask the Divine to reveal your Life Purpose to you. It is surprising how quickly the answer shall be given unto you.

Whether you already know why you are here or you are still waiting to find out, always remember, life is a Journey. Enjoy it. A quote attributed to Eleanor Roosevelt reminds us to live our best life in the moment. It is as follows:

Yesterday is History

Tomorrow is a Mystery

Today is a Gift

That is why we call it the Present.

Acknowledgements

I wish to give my sincere thanks to----

My parents for everything they have ever done for me.

My husband Daniel for his never ending love and support.

My sons, daughters in laws and grandchildren for listening to my stories of the Old Days.

Angeline King for her encouraging words while editing this book.

Ian Hooper and Book Reality for publishing it for me.

My beautiful neighbour for never losing faith in me and giving me gorgeous flowers.

My dear friends Sheila and Ernie who brought so much love and laughter into our family.

All of our wonderful family and friends who gave us love and support when we needed it most.

Kenny Corris, Raye Bower and Anne-Lise Erikson for being a fine example of everything a Healer should be.

Brian Lynch and John Spence for their wisdom,

their love and the laughter we share.

All those who work continually for the good of others on the Earth.

Finally, to the reader for taking the time to read my book. I wish you Joy wherever you are on the Spiritual Path.

About The Author

Always looking for something challenging to stimulate her mind Morna Croft decided to do a creative writing workshop at the age of sixty. Having a couple of stories printed gave her the confidence to write her memoir. She chose to work under a pseudonym to protect the privacy of her family.

In her first book, *Beyond the Sallagh Braes* she tells the story of her life, from her childhood on a farm in the Antrim Hills to travelling the world with her husband.

Finding out that she was a healer while living in Spain, Morna realised that another book would be necessary to explain the Spiritual Journey she found herself on and so came, *Many Paths up the Mountain*.

Morna lives in a beautiful seaside village on the Antrim coast with her husband Daniel. They share their home often with family and friends. Her interests are Angels, healing, crystals, reading, writing, art and travel. She is also a summer gardener.

Morna Croft's Email address is:
mornacroft@gmail.com

www.ingramcontent.com/pod-product-compliance
Lightning Source LLC
Chambersburg PA
CBHW030259100526
44590CB00012B/449